# ALASKA

## *ONE MORE TIME*

# TRUE ADVENTURES

RED AND ROSE LUSK
FIRST EDITION 2004

First Edition First Printing 2004

Book design by Red Lusk

Printed in the United States of America

ISBN 0-9759188-0-X
Library of Congress Cataloging-in-Publication Data

For more information: Contact our website
http://www.alaskaonemoretime.com/

*We dedicate this book to "Bud"*

*and his unknowing contribution in the writing of this book.*

*Without him and his urging, we may have never made that first trip.*

*BUD*

*Bud died in August 1990.*

Rosemarie Lusk

 

 

This is the author's first attempt at writing. Each chapter is from Rosemarie's journal which corresponds to individual trips her and her husband, Jerry (Red), made to Alaska. She is a Registered Nurse and continues to work in her field of Emergency Nursing on a part-time basis.

# CONTENTS

# PREFACE

We have made ten journeys to Alaska, and each had different stories to tell. These "stories" were sent to friends and family in the form of a "log" of our daily adventures. Over the years I have had much encouragement to write this book so others could share in the journey. I've focused mainly on our favorite areas in Alaska and tried to be as accurate as possible. If you find in your travels to Alaska that I have made errors, please write and tell me as I am already planning a second edition and would appreciate any feedback. I hope this adventure will make your trip even better. Maybe for the first time, or perhaps…

ALASKA ONE MORE TIME

Red and Rose
c/o R & R Enterprise
5224 Kings Mill Rd.
#210
Mason, OH  45040
Or e-mail redrose@alaskaonemoretime.com

# ACKNOWLEDGEMENTS

This is my first attempt at writing, and the project could have never been realized without the help of my husband and daughter.

To my husband Jerry (Red), in setting up my office, so I would have a quiet place to write. Thank you for all the hours of searching for just the right pictures that were needed to help convey our story. Your design of the "Book Cover", gives a preview of the adventures within. Thank you also, for the many hours in your search for just the right printer/publisher to complete our project. Most of all, thank you for your continued encouragement and patience. THANK YOU.

To my daughter, Carla Gzym, for your time spent in designing my computer needs for this project. I was a computer novice and I'm sure you wanted to lose your patience with me on more than one occasion. Thank you for your assistance by putting it in the proper electronic format for the printer. Thank you for establishing and designing the website. I could not have completed the writing of this adventure without you. THANK YOU.

Many thanks also to my friends and family whose encouragement and faith in me made this all possible.

# INTRODUCTION

Alaska is a landscape of "Majestic Wilderness", and to travel there is a dream of a lifetime. We wrote this book of our true adventures so others may share the many experiences that we had.

For all those who make this unforgettable trip, you will be left with life long memories of the most spectacular scenery in the world.

Alaska offers something for everyone; be it viewing wildlife, fishing for the elusive salmon or photographing its' magnificent wonders. To visit some of Alaska's quaint towns is like stepping back in time.

Traveling to Alaska is a true adventure not only once, but for many…

ALASKA ONE MORE TIME

# THE FIRST JOURNEY

June 15, 1984, "Alaska here we come". We left in our 1979 Chevrolet pickup with a tall truck cap that Jerry had converted to include a bed and plenty of storage.

OUR HOME FOR THE NEXT MONTH

The excitement and anticipation in planning our first trip was like a young child awaiting the arrival of Santa Claus. The decision to go this year came about with an unexpected event in our lives. Jerry (also known as Red) had a heart attack approximately 6 weeks earlier and at age 48. We felt the need to slow down our lives and travel while able to do so. Our friend Bud's urging sunk in and trip planning began. We first met Bud and his wife Jackie, when we moved to Florida in early 1981. They were both long time residents of Alaska, and spent their winters in Florida.

I took a month's leave from my job (not long enough as we soon found out) and continued to make plans to leave. We were packed to the top, including extra tires due to the stories of previous Alaska travelers and their encounters with multiple tire problems. We felt quite comfortable with all our preparations, including the purchase of the *Alaska Milepost,* a must-have guide for our first trip. Mandy, our small poodle and official mascot, would also be accompanying us.

We left our home in Pine Island, Florida and stopped to say goodbye to John our friend who owned the Gulf Breeze, a local restaurant and bar. Many friends were there to see us off on our adventure which made departing a little tearful. They gave us a five dollar bill with all their names written on it, instructing us to buy a beer in Alaska on them. We finally broke away, stopped for gas and took fried chicken out of cooler to put up front with us. We plan on eating while driving. It's really raining hard as we head north towards Interstate 75 and Punta Gorda, Florida.

Don't think reality has hit me that we are actually doing this. It was hard to leave work today knowing that I will not see everyone for such a long time. Jerry is in his glory when he is behind the wheel with the radio playing. Our destination tonight is Interstate 10 before shutting down for a good nights sleep. We have this deal that we take turns cooking and tonight it's his turn. We are eating the chicken that I prepared ahead. I don't think this is working out just right.

By 8:10 pm we've eaten our supper and completely devoured the fudge Cathy (nurse from work) made for us. If I can't fit through the cab window to the camper, I'll blame Cathy for the extra pounds. Not even two hours into the trip and truck is a mess! Chicken is all over and we can't find a rest area with a potty, so we use our "porta potty". We must have put it together wrong, because it leaked out in the wrong places.....at this rate we will need a car wash (an internal one). It has stopped raining and we are almost to Ruskin, Florida.

Short of Ruskin, Florida we stopped for a cup of coffee and gas. I'm sleepy and Jerry is wide awake so we keep on trucking. I finally go in the back and try to sleep. Jerry pushes on and gives up just north of Perry, Florida...Good night to all.

Saturday, June 16, 7:45 am. Woke up to a glorious morning. We traveled 336 miles yesterday spending the evening in a rest area. Guess I'll try my hand at using the camp stove to make coffee. My "handyman' is still sleeping. So if it gets made I guess it's up to me. Mandy, being her usual good self, is surveying my attempts at brewing coffee. Staff at work gave me a coffee pot as a going away gift, which I'm putting to use this morning. Guess who finally wakes up to the rich aroma?

We found a hose leaking antifreeze and had to haul out the tools.....we're not even out of the state of Florida.

Just east of Mobile, Alabama, we stop and lunched on cold sliced beef sandwiches and ice tea. Cooler is holding ice real good. Truck is heating up a bit, not sure why. We're guessing it might be the thermostat. The sky is bright blue with big puffy clouds. The terrain is much like Michigan with rolling hills and miles of big trees.

After taking a nap, we feel refreshed and head towards Gulfport, Mississippi. Our route will eventually turn northwest to Jackson, Mississippi. The highway consists of causeway bridges and the landscape is getting flatter. The truck still heats up at intervals and we plan to try and find a Chevrolet dealer once we turn off Interstate 10 on to Highway 49. The truck is also burning more than the usual amount of oil...poor lizzy. She just got a clean bill of health from the truck doctor. The temperature here is very hot...88 degrees plus as we cross another time zone and gain an hour. Local time is 4:50 pm. Just stopped for gas again and truck seems to be ok, although Jerry thinks the timing is out of whack. We're heading for Jackson, Mississippi. This is beautiful country; rolling hills, big trees, lots of pines, rust clay ground and beautiful homes of red brick. We still prefer the old houses with their southern charm, tilting porches and patched roofs. The characteristics seem to shout, "In here lives real hard working down to earth people".

At 6:30 pm Jerry takes his turn at cooking. Easy out again. He opts for McDonalds.

After our fast food feast, we head into downtown Jackson, Mississippi. The towering peaks of taller buildings stand in a haze. The combination of high temps and humidity seem to engulf them. Jackson is a big city with a tangle of freeways and a frenzy of traffic. Our plans are to drive to Vicksburg, Mississippi, then north on the Interstate along the Mississippi River, where we hope to find a camp area for the evening. Surprisingly the truck is doing better.

Sunday, June 17. We traveled 556 miles yesterday, stopped at Vicksburg and toured the Vicksburg National Military Park. We stayed at a KOA park. The shower felt good and even plugged in the little TV to watch a movie. I took my first pictures with the new 35 mm camera we purchased for this trip. After we crossed the Mississippi River the land became flat with a lot of farm land. We passed pecan tree farms. The habitants here are either real rich or real poor folks. At 10:30 am we head north of State Road 65 to Tallulah, Louisiana. It's so obvious that a form of slavery still exists here, we'll go by the lowest value in housing and then a quarter mile later we'll see a beautiful brick mansion and this cycle repeats itself. We're on a two lane road where we really see the south and all the uniqueness that the area presents.

There's an interesting garbage service here. Occasionally, we'll see people from all the side roads bringing garbage to the main road for pickup at a local dumpster. Seems odd they'd be doing this on a lovely Sunday morning.

Shortly after noon we get back on State Road 65. The terrain consists of nothing but beans, pecans and rice fields. We never realized they grew rice in the United States. The river is banked up all along with high mountains of soil; very few businesses are open – no shopping centers or bars, mainly just eating places and a few gas stations. It's very hot and Mandy just gave up her dinner on Jerry's side of the seat and he's acting like the world is coming to an end. He is also anxious to get to the mountains and cooler weather. We are headed for Pine Bluff, Arkansas.

Lunch today consisted of peaches purchased at local roadside stand. They were so good. Heading out of Pine Bluff the landscape changes to that of, you guessed it, pine trees. We meander through rolling hills again. The temperature is 88 degrees, sunny and hazy. We are on Interstate 40 thirty miles east of Fort Smith, Arkansas. Stopped for beer to put in cooler and guess what? No beer or liquor sales in the state of Arkansas on Sunday. Jerry is having a fit and we have approximately 147 miles to Oklahoma, sure hope they sell beer. It is very hot and hazy and we've run into some small mountains, the Ozarks. Guess who is due for a nap? So guess I'm going to do some driving.

The temperature at 7 pm is a squelching 90 degrees. We're in Oklahoma now, approximately 130 miles east of Oklahoma City. The terrain is very hilly. We're on Interstate 40 and will stay at a rest area just east of the city. We plan on having the truck checked tomorrow. My turn to cook and we'll have sliced beef, pork and beans, chips and fudge for a finish, sounds like a well balanced diet? Oh yes, we finally got to buy beer. We munched on the caramel pop corn all day. Another of Cathy's treats. The soil here looks very rich and a lot of irrigation is noticeable. Wildflowers dot the roadside in pastel hues. As we pass the town of Henrietta, Oklahoma our scenery turns from flowers to that of pumping oil wells. As the sun sets, the temperature drops and we cool off a bit. Strangely, we haven't read or heard any news for several days and really don't miss it.

Monday, June 18. By my calculations we drove 510 miles yesterday. We spent the night in a beautiful rest area high on a hill. The winds blew through the windows all night. We slept good and got started down the highway today at 8:50. Made coffee before departing and filled the thermos for the morning. We stopped at a Buick dealer in Shawnee and that's where I'm writing from now. We are sitting in the garage while they are finding out what ails lizzy. Mandy's all mixed up in deciding which guy she wants to bite first, so we're sitting in the camper and she is laying looking out the window checking everyone out. The weather is much cooler here, but it feels good.

Jerry wanted to get a motel last night, but I convinced him to wait a few more days. We really are doing ok! Its fun to see just how much you can do without. We wash our face and brush our teeth in the rest area facilities and it's so nice to just be natural. I'm not wearing any make-up and Jerry hasn't shaven since we left. He states he isn't going to until he gets back home, but I don't think he'll do it. We are very comfortable in our camper; he did such a nice job furnishing it. We both are well except Jerry's "tennis elbow" is still bothering him. With truck repairs complete, we're back on the road again. Seems the timing was off. Total charges… $14.40.

Off in the distance we see tall buildings which landmarks Oklahoma City. Weather is cool and raining a little. The traffic picks up as we get closer to the city. Guess what? Truck still isn't running right. We stopped and pulled the bug screen off the front, thinking that's what is making her heat up. We stopped at an auto accessory store across from Tinker Air Force and purchased spark plugs. We'll have them on hand if they are needed.

The traffic system here is different, instead of exits, they call them gates! And all you see around here is men in "Air Force green". Donna (a nurse from work) would be in seventh heaven here.

We just left Oklahoma City, it's been quite a day. Lizzy got worse so we stopped in a shopping mall and Jerry changed the spark plugs while I went grocery shopping. At the checkout, I handed the clerk a $50.00 bill and she gave me back $5.80 in change for a $14.20 grocery bill. I informed her of the mistake. Well, to make a long story short the police were called, couldn't find the $50.00 bill and told me I could hire a lawyer. I pretty much told them what they could do and I was out $30.00. Boy you talk about the price of groceries going up! They are sure high in Oklahoma. As it is too expensive in Oklahoma for us, we head for Amarillo, Texas. The skies are dark and spooky towards our destination. Appears we're heading from one bad experience into another.

By 4:25 pm we are in the midst of a bad storm. Besides heavy traffic, we have to contend with strong winds, rain, lightening and zero visibility. This day makes you want to go back to bed and start over. And as for the sparks plugs… Jerry replaced 4 of the 8. Didn't we just have new ones put in? Good news is that the truck seems to run better now. Fifteen miles from the Texas line and the sun starts to shine again. The earth here is deep reddish brown, rolling hills, very few trees, only sage brush and tumble weeds which you can see for miles.

We went through some areas that looked like a miniature Grand Canyon. The land became flat, almost as if we crossed through an invisible wall. The road is real bumpy now and there's a lack of scenery. Besides lots of cattle the landscape lacks trees, houses and it's starting to get cold. We now have our windows up and vents closed and if it's like this tomorrow we'll trade shorts for jeans. We begin seeing mile after mile of nothing but corn and wheat fields. We are about 30 miles east of Amarillo, Texas. Off in the far distance we can see a nuclear plant. All the highways in Texas have service roads. Just heard on the radio that it is 65 degrees. We've gone from 90 to 65 in a very short time. As fast as the city appeared out of no where, it disappeared in the same manner.

We are now heading north on 287. It's raining and we are back into rolling hills. Nothing but tumble weed and sage brush. No houses in sight for as far as you can see.

June 19. We traveled 418 miles yesterday. Our host campground for the evening was the Dumas, Texas KOA. The hot shower and clean bedding felt so good. They call this a campground but it's no more than a farmer's field. A clay one at that! If it rains I don't think we'll ever get out. They say they grow them big in Texas! Well they do, there was the biggest toad in the bath house that I've ever seen. Woke up to a temperature of 60, Jerry switched to long pants and I still have shorts on. Sun is shining brightly as we head for New Mexico. It is so sparsely populated here that if you visit a neighbor plan on it being a whole day's event. It takes a half a day to get there, another to return home.

We are in New Mexico now and we gained another hour. Off in the distance you can see the foothills starting to form the mountain range. It's cool and I may have to change into jeans also.

11:00 am and we are about 30 miles from US 25, still in New Mexico and just got our first glimpse of the Rockies. They're snow covered and breath taking, (I wish all of you could be here to see this site), our whole front seat is occupied with binoculars and camera equipment.

Just came into Colorado; ears are popping with the changes in altitude. We are back on freeway and winding in and around the mountains and they are covered with pine trees and some are barren rock. Sun is shining brightly now, but it is still cold. Jerry just informed me that we have come 2000 miles. You can actually see it snow on the mountain peaks and yet where we are it's probably in the low 70's. The mountains are majestic, luring and yet forbidden. They are unlike any other part of the world. We are just south of Colorado Springs and Pikes Peak is in view but hazy. Next city is Denver.

5:30 pm we came through Denver, traffic like Chicago...We've just turned off into Loveland and will stop and stock up before heading into Rocky Mountain National Park.

We did our grocery shopping and now we are winding our way through Big Thompson Canyon and on to Estes Park. Jerry's turn for supper and he is taking me out and then we'll find a campground for the night. I have jeans and a long sleeve shirt on and it is getting colder.

June 20, traveled 420 miles yesterday, just passed a sign that we are at 14,250 feet. We stayed at a campground in the Rockies last night, high on a mountain, cold but good sleeping. I fixed bacon and eggs on the camp stove, and we started through the park and saw big horn sheep and took pictures; we are really seeing nature at its best. This road winds around the mountain ledge with no guard rails. My every nerve has been tested to the max. Just took a walk through the snow and reminded us of how much we love warm weather. We are still climbing and there are banks of snow 12 feet high, it's unreal, so beautiful that words can't describe. It's a little hard to breath, took picture of a glacier and took some real cute pictures of Jerry feeding something that looked like a woodchuck.

We stopped at the visitor center for coffee and saw an elk off in the distance. We're now driving down and have 22 miles downhill, a lot of travelers here in this area and it is only open 2 to 3 months a year. Guess what? We ran into a snow storm. We're winding around the mountain cliffs on slippery roads and I wish I was in Pine Island right about now. I'm writing this as we angle our way down. Snow is still 4 to 6 feet deep. Just saw a deer; beautiful but moved out of range to quickly to take a picture. We are now traveling the valley before we continue our descent. Just came through the southwest end of the park, sun is shining, but still cool and just finished lunch. Lizzy seems to tolerate the mountain driving so far. We are now headed west on State Road 40 to Craig, Colorado, there are no ski areas open so far. Jerry says "no way is he going rafting in this **! x"**!! weather.

Finally got pictures of Ma, Pa and Baby Elk. We are following along side of the Colorado River. It's very high and swift. It took six hours to get through the park and it's snowing again and the heater is on in the truck. At 4:00 pm we came into Steamboat Springs ski area. There are hundreds of condominiums nestled in the mountains, but no skiing though! Still driving northwest. Just stopped and looked at a herd of antelope. Beautiful creatures! I could watch them all day. The mountains are taking on a different character now, not as high and have cover of what appears to be green sage brush.

Still driving on, we're going by a strange formation of mountains. I can see why they are part of the Dinosaur National Park; they look like the backs of dinosaurs. We crossed into Utah about 7:30 and will start looking for a campground. We have not stayed in a motel yet. Jerry has wanted to, but he does pretty well with the camping and I love it. I love the nature and there is beauty everywhere you look.

We found a nice campground just south of Flaming Gorge National Park and we'll go there tomorrow. It will be difficult or impossible to surpass today. We are watching the movie *Somewhere in Time* filmed on Mackinaw Island. It's really interesting because we've been there several times even stayed at the Grand Hotel. Mackinaw Island is in Michigan.

June 21, traveled 317 miles yesterday, woke up to another beautiful morning, fixed coffee outside and wrote a few post cards. Jerry still hasn't shaven and claims he isn't going to. Had to back track to town to buy a new coffee pot, the glass one cracked. We just came upon a real cattle round up. Looks like a large herd broke out of the fence and cowboys on horses were rounding them up from the highway. It's a beautiful day, cool but sunny. We are climbing up a very steep grade and mountains are changing again into jagged rock formation. There are signs telling of a prehistoric era, such as dinosaurs, petrified forest, and fossils of crocodile, squid, and fish all in the same area, really interesting.

We still have snow on the mountain tops, but not on the road any more. When we were in Rocky Mountain National Park we were about 10,000 feet, driving on the ridge in a road construction area. Jerry was getting awful close to the edge and I yelled at him and he said he didn't want to get over any more because there was a 6" drop between the old and the new pavement, I said I couldn't be concerned (not really how I said it) about his 6" drop when I had a 10,000 foot drop on my side.

The mountains are now covered with pines and poplar trees and for miles and miles the pines have been attacked by beetles. We stopped at canyon of Flaming Gorge, so beautiful and so different again from other mountains we've seen. The people running the visitor center were from Traverse City, Michigan. The gorge consists of different layers of colored rock, yellow, red, and black. Now and then Jerry gets yelled at to slow down, were descending now and you can smell the brakes, (he says it's because they are new). I think he's not really wanting me to be worried.

We stopped by a rushing stream and drank cold, clear water. Also filled our water jugs and had lunch of crackers, milk, lunchmeat, cheese and peanut butter cookies. Just came into Wyoming and came upon more cowboys rounding up cattle in the middle of the highway. We have really enjoyed taking these back roads. Soon we will be on Interstate 80 and we've decided to go to Salt Lake City, Utah and then take Interstate 15 north to Butte, Montana. Jerry just stopped and picked me a bouquet of lavender flowers that look just like orchids. Here it is the first day of summer and up here the leaves, flowers and fields are just coming alive. Came across another cattle roundup and this time got a picture. The cattle have very heavy coats for the cold weather. Changed our mind again and decided to stick with first plan, crossed over 80 and continued on 412 to 189 and over to 30. Just took a picture of a pair of antelope in Carter, Wyoming.

4:20 pm and we're just crossing into Idaho, caught a glimpse of the majestic Teton Mountains, north about 140 miles. It is a real crisp sunny day which allows a view of the snow capped range. I'm really enjoying the new camera and I'll have to borrow a bank loan to develop all the film.

Coming into Pocatello, Idaho where we will get back on Interstate 15 and continue north. We'll try and find a rest area tonight and start out early in am for Coeur d'Alene, Idaho and maybe find a cabin in the mountains for the weekend to do laundry and rest up before heading into British Columbia. Several hours ago we noticed the front windshield had 2 cracks in it and we haven't even got to the Alaskan Highway yet.

We decided to stay in a KOA again, cooked supper and took a hot shower and retired for the night. We have driven 378 miles today.

June 22, it was so cold last night, even 2 blankets didn't do the job, and even the dog was under the covers. Got up at 6 am and headed for a coffee shop. First time that we didn't made coffee in the morning. People here are in winter coats. It's 7:45 am and headed north to Butte, Montana and just heard on the radio that it is now 50 degrees. Sun is out bright, snow on the mountains. To back track, yesterday we saw an antelope tangled in a barbwire fence, dead and also a mother sheep that just gave birth. We are really seeing the animal life. The mountains we're traveling through now are covered again with sagebrush; peaks are rounded with just traces of snow. The higher elevation ones are covered with snow. We are in Montana now and the fields are filled with cattle and it's a strange picture to see cattle and antelope in same area. Just stopped at rest area for nature break, picked some lilacs which are just starting to bloom, everyday the cab of the truck has different flowers. We're going through an area that's flooded out, the river is very swift and the banks are all under water. We're trying something new, we have a 12 volt coffee pot that we've had for years. We used to take it to motels. It has an adapter for the cigarette lighter so here goes.

Jerry's beard is about a quarter inch, hasn't shaved since we left. 10:20 and coffee is done and tasted great. We passed the Continental Divide, once again, and Interstate 90 is just up the road. We've had sweaters and jackets on all morning, windows closed and heater running. Stopped for gas and strange to see everyone in heavy jackets on June 22, we turned off 90 onto Alternate 10 and will take this back to 90 again. We are now in a heavy forest of pines, what a picture as we wind around the mountains and see snow capped mountains, clear streams and lakes. You think were kidding about the cold! We saw horses in the fields with horse blankets on. Jerry says he brought a fly swatter and I don't know what for, no fly could survive up here.

This trip to Alaska has been a life time dream of ours and we wish that each and every one of you that have the same dream, get it fulfilled. So much of what we see and experience can't be put into words, it's a feeling that one gets and at times indescribable of the beauty of the mountains, a rushing river, the wild flowers, the wild animals and yes, even the terrible roads. It makes you wonder about the conditions that the men were under in the making of the "Alaskan Highway."

We stopped to stretch and have another cup of coffee and take another nature break. We are back on Interstate 90 heading west to Missoula, Montana. Sun is out but still cold. All the rivers and creeks in this area are overflowing their banks from the snow runoff. The last time we were through this area was January 1977 and it's not much warmer now. Had salami sandwiches and milk for lunch and we had the best view in town through the windshield of the truck. We still plan to find a spot on a stream in the mountains and stay put for a few days to catch up with the "truck lag."

Jerry states that we've just come 3300 miles and we are on Interstate 90, 165 miles east of Spokane, Washington.

We are at Wallace, Idaho, the town is decorated red, white and blue and it's their 100th anniversary. The temperature is 52 degrees and we wish we had just a little of Florida weather. The area that we are going through is still very dense pines and high mountains. We are 47 miles from where we want to stay for a few days. We gained another hour; its 5 pm and we are now in Coeur d'Alene, Idaho. This area is nestled around a lake and river of the same name. Jerry is in the bank exchanging some US money for Canadian money, they are paying 31 cents on the dollar, so for every $100.00 US you get $131.00 Canadian dollars, not bad, huh? We found a charming little A-frame cabin on Lake Pend Oreille.

The Lake is 50 miles long, nestled by mountains and the lake is very deep, 1100 feet in some areas. We traveled 555 miles today and we will stay here till Sunday afternoon and then head north to British Columbia. We are just going to relax for the next couple of days, do laundry, clean up the truck and get our selves ready to push on. The next day we decided to explore the area, ate breakfast out and found a laundromat (first time for doing the laundry). Sun is shining brightly and it is fairly warm. The trees are all budded out. This is apparently a German settlement around a French lake, different yes? We explored further and found a floating lounge and checked it out, it was also a marina and all the docks here "float", real different. We're going out for dinner to the "Trestle Inn" their special a prime rib on Saturday and we reached our saturation point of camp food. Jerry and Mandy are catching up with their naps.

THE IDAHO REST STOP

Sunday June 24th and we woke up at 7:20…with headaches. Jerry and I went for dinner but never got to the eating part. We were introduced to "Steel" a clear alcohol that when served over ice tastes really good. We had a lot of fun (but not this morning). The staff and other diners at the Trestle Inn were very friendly and we had a great time.

Today we start out again and push on to Alaska. 10:30 am left the cabin, sun is out, and warm and I even put shorts on. Stopped and stocked up with groceries. We will be entering Canada soon, traveling on State Road 95 heading for Bonners Ferry. We entered British Columbia at 12:50 pm. Customs was easy, questions asked were "do you have any firearms?" And when we said no they would repeat the same question again and ask "are you sure?" They asked for Mandy's papers and asked it we had any fruit and that was it.

We are in a real dense forest with mountains on all sides, heading for Cranbrook, British Columbia and Highways 93 and 95. It got a lot colder and we are now traveling through Kootenay National Park. We already have seen two different groups of mountain goats, hot springs and high snow topped mountains. It is really beautiful here. It is 6 pm and it's getting darker, just took a picture of a large elk. We are now in Banff and it's getting a lot colder. 7 pm and now we are at Lake Louise perhaps the most beautiful area in the world. We are at a primitive campground, camping at its best, pit toilets, no electric and way out in the woods. We were warned about the bears and hope we see some. Ate chili for supper and retired early, mainly just to keep warm. We are at the base of the mountains and the mountains are covered with snow. We traveled 298 miles today.

June 25th, started out at 7:45, making coffee in the 12 volt pot as we go. It's a crisp morning, sun but snow everywhere. This part of the country is very, very beautiful, but forbidden in ways and gives you a kind of lonely feeling, maybe because it's foreign to us. It's almost as if God set this part of the world aside for the animals. We stopped for a break and had coffee and toast. We are now in the highest mountains we've ever been in. In areas where the snow is melting it provides many rushing falls. Jerry has on his "Old Bastards Shirt" which represents the IOOB Club…International Order Of Old Bastards and it has aroused questions from strangers who get quite a chuckle out of it. The snow is getting deeper at lower altitudes now and is within our reach. We have on jeans, sweaters and jackets. Stopped for gas and found that the temperature is 40 degrees, no wonder we are cold.

Just came upon big horn sheep in the road and also saw another large elk with his horns in the velvet. So far the roads, parks, direction signs, and food places have been excellent. Everything is very new and very clean. There are a lot of people traveling this stretch from all over. I'd like to have the money that's spent in camping rigs and all the gear, including all the camera equipment.

We came through Jasper and now we are headed west on Highway 16 to Prince George. It's half rain and half snow. We have gone through 3 national parks since we left the US border. As we enter Mount Robinson Park, I was informed that we now have come 4000 miles. You don't see any liter anywhere. We just finished lunch and I think we take for granted our panoramic view. 1:10 pm we are at one of the highest mountain in the Canadian Rockies, Mt. Robinson. I think we're even getting used to all the snow. Strange, the further north we go it's getting a little warmer and now we get a glimpse of roadside flowers and there are some houses once in a while. The mountains are less rocky and have trees on them and even less snow.

BIG HORN SHEEP

MOUNT ROBINSON IN BRITISH COLUMBIA

We stopped and filled with gas, next station is 91 miles down the road. We are having fun converting kilometers to miles. Here everything is km. This area has fertile soil, huge cedar trees and very thick underbrush. School is still in session, maybe they have the winter instead of summer off. Jerry just picked some wild daisies. We have gone through areas that have been burnt for miles up and down the mountain sides.

We just saw our first moose and were able to get a picture, thank goodness for the zoom lens. Here's another first, we came to a construction zone and before we could continue we had to be escorted by a "pilot car", so here was a woman driver in a pick-up with the sign on her door "White Lady Pilot Service", so we went 35 miles an hour through the best construction zone we have ever seen. Jerry was screaming all the time, but I'm sure the lady felt important as she paraded a line of traffic from one end of a 2 mile stretch to the other. You talk about creating a job!

THE ALASKAN HIGHWAY IN 1984

THE FAMOUS PILOT CAR

ALASKA HERE WE COME

We arrived in Prince George, one of the largest cities in British Columbia. We entered Highway 97 to Dawson Creek through a wooden bridge that I really didn't think would hold us. It seemed that once we crossed the bridge we left civilization behind. We now have our first taste of gravel roads and for the next 13 miles we saw vehicles that were covered with dirt, oh well…Dawson Creek, here we come! The trees in this area are just starting to bud. There are mile after mile of lavender flowers along the roadside. It's 5:30 pm but the sun is where you would expect it should be at 2 pm. I just got another bouquet of flowers, beautiful red and lavender ones. 6:30 pm and we are really in the north woods, there is nothing but cedar and pine and frequently we meet up with huge trucks loaded with logs. This is bear country, and sure hope we see one.

Jerry's turn to cook; and guess what he did again? Yup! Ate out in a little log cabin in the middle of no where and they gave us twice as much as we needed and very reasonable. We have about 80 miles to our stop for the night. It's still very light at 8:45 pm. We stopped to let Mandy out and were introduced to the mosquitoes that we have heard so much about. We've just come upon road construction again and this time it's rough, dusty. Winds whip around the mountains and the visibility is not poor. We drove to the campground listed in the *Milepost* and it looked like a toss between MacDonald's farm and Joe's junkyard, so we decided to drive on. We never found any place and drove on through the night to Dawson Creek. We came to the top of a hill where we could see the city in the distance. We pulled off in a little gravel turn off and decided to stay for the night at 11:45 pm. We had not been to bed very long when an old, loud truck stopped and what sounded like a bunch of drunks just sat there for a while. We were really concerned and decided not to take any chances. I crawled through the slide window and started the truck and drove into town dragging Mandy's dog chain behind. It had been tied on the back bumper. We then parked in a store parking lot and I didn't get any sleep the rest of the night.

Woke up a 4:50 am it was as light as could be. The town is reminiscing of an old mining town. The ratio of men to women is about 6 to 1 and when we went for coffee I felt like I was on display; it was a very uncomfortable feeling. We are going to have lizzy checked one more time before we head up the Alaskan highway. We drove 631 miles yesterday.

It's a very cloudy day and cool. Timing was off on the truck. We are at a shopping center getting supplies for the last 1500 miles and there are other campers doing the same. It gives you kind of a scared feeling, like you were going to some unknown place. I wonder if this is how people felt that first set out with wagons across the west. If you want to know the truth, right now I'd give anything to be back in Florida. Jerry is trying to buy some screen to put on the front of the truck; the bugs up here are terrible.

We left Dawson Creek (Gateway to the Alaska Highway). The start of the Alcan Highway begins here at mile marker 0. The fertile, rich soil, attributes to the abundant crops in this area. The road is paved but very rough. The terrain is rolling hills and very green. It's kind of nice to be out of the mountains for a change.

MILE MARKER "0" STARTS HERE

June 26, and we just came through Taylor's Landing over a very long and old bridge suspended high above a river. We stopped at a rest area (mile post 80) and

18

talked with some people traveling from Minnesota who were on their way to Alaska also. We met vehicles going the opposite way that were covered with mud, makes one wonder what lies ahead. My bouquet of the day is a combination of small blue bell and the largest dandelions I've every seen.

We've just had our pilot service again for a couple of miles. We also were informed that we have 450 miles of gravel in British Columbia, so I'm covering everything up with plastic. I'd like to get a hold of the person that told us we only had 90 miles of gravel. An oil tanker just came towards us throwing stones and we now have another chip in our window.

Now we are traveling through an area that has been burnt for miles, and we're starting to see big mountains in the distance. The gravel stretch we're on now is for 70 miles and still on very rugged roads. I can see this is going to be an endurance test for both of us and we're just starting. We may take the ferry back to Seattle. You have to see the road to believe it, there is only a strip in the middle that is passable and there is a truck about ¾ of a mile ahead and all you can see is dust.

We are getting closer to snow capped mountains again and I'm already a nervous wreck in wondering what kind of roads are on those mountains. We have to drive with our lights on the dust is so bad I think if we were smart we'd turn back. And to think we have 1360 miles to go before we get to Bud and Jackie's.

Waiting for the pilot car again; this is stupid. We've driven over 4000 miles over some of the worst mountain roads and now we need a pilot! The only pilot I'd like to see is with United Airlines. The pavement is a little better than the gravel you can see for miles and miles as we drive the ridges, it is really raining now and makes driving even more dangerous. We have come about 222 miles since we left Dawson Creek. We haven't even seen any wild life. 3:45 pm and we are about 35 miles from Fort Nelson and we're getting a motel there to rest up before heading on tomorrow. The area we're going through is marshy and pine covered. We've been driving through a valley and on flat roads for quite a while. We are so tired that it's hard to find any beauty in this area at all. We found a motel and we'll shut down, we have come 288 miles (a little slower going now).

June 26, Boy! Did we enjoy the motel (better, it cost $50.00) I must have soaked in the tub for an hour, watched TV and slept in. We went for coffee and toast and headed out at 9:45 am. It rained during the night so guess that means we get mud instead of dust today. Sun is out, temperature is around 60 degrees and it is 332 miles to Watson Lake in the Yukon, and almost all of it is gravel. It's 10:20 am and we have been waiting for 10 minutes for one of our "pilot cars". 10:40 still on gravel roads and very rough, the big trucks come by and throw rocks and mud. It's a good thing that both Jerry and I wanted to take this trip, because right about now we would be cussing the other out if it wasn't a joint venture. We are already discussing taking the ship back from Alaska to Washington.

The scenery is very hilly and tree covered with pines and poplars. Stopped for a nature break and the mosquitoes almost carried us away.

Sun is out brightly now and we stopped at a café and gas station combined (the only one for a hundred miles). We continue to wind our way through steep rough roads around the mountains with drop-offs straight down for what seems like miles. Scenery is getting more interesting, more like what we had imagined it would be. We are on a stretch of paved road and came upon 6 horses in the road all with bells on their necks. We've heard that they have a lot of wild mustangs here. It's getting cooler as we get into mountains with snow again.

Just came upon mountain goats in the road eating the salt from winter road maintenance. We are now on a high ridge following a river below. The flower for today is wild pink roses. It has taken 3 ½ hours to go 100 miles and we only used ¼ tank of gas. 2:45 pm and we arrive at beautiful Muncho Lake, which is surrounded by mountains. The lake is a blue/green color caused by the zinc oxide (we were told). We stopped at a very unique log cabin, run by a young German couple that specialized in all homemade pastries, bread and other homemade cooking. We bought more than our share.

At 801 km in the *Milepost*, we stopped at Laird Hot Springs, a beautiful natural hot springs located about ¼ mile back in the woods. The springs are reached by a wooden boardwalk and there was also a primitive campground. We walked back to see the springs but didn't take our suits. There were a lot of people soaking in 100 degree plus water. We didn't spend much time there which in later years proved to be one of our favorite stops. Saw a moose and really enjoyed the walk, maybe we walked off a few pounds. The area was posted with "Warning Bears in Area" but we saw none.

Heading on the trail again, still very bumpy and road is full of large chuck holes. Every so often you see bits and pieces of car parts; we have met some vehicles that looked like they went through a rock slide. The area that we're in is mile after mile of an old burn that occurred in 1982. It was the 2nd largest fire in Yukon history. These roads get on your nerves after a while and to think I gave up the flats of Pine Island. We are still going through the burn area and it wasn't till 7:10 pm that we finally got out. Jerry informs me that we have come 5000 miles and we are 33 miles from Watson Lake, Yukon Territory.

8:45 pm and just came to Watson Lake, a real primitive area, dirt roads, mostly native people and famous for "The Sign Post Area". This is an area on the highway where people from all over the world have left signs of towns, states and cities.

SIGN POST FOREST IN WATSON LAKE

Campground we were headed for was full of a lot of dirty vehicles, including ours. Stopped for a drink in a local lounge. I ordered a margarita and Jerry ordered a whisky and 7-up and the tab was $7.25 (remember this was 1984). We went down the road 3 or 4 miles to a government campground ($5.00) and the mosquitoes were terrible. We spent the night but, cooked and ate inside. As I write this it is 10:45 pm and as light as can be. We are about 1/3$^{rd}$ of the way on the Alaskan highway and we have come through some terrible roads (take that back; trails). This trip sure is a test for survival of the fittest. We left the campsite at 8 am; the bumpy roads have made Mandy very nervous. Today we start out on pavement that is good in comparison to what we have had. Sun is out but, it's quite cool and we are in sweaters and jeans. Stopped for coffee at a typical mountain cabin and talked with a lot of other travelers and the bus driver of a tour group. He stated we have covered the worst of the roads. In our conversation with other travelers; everyone has their own version of how bad or how good the trip has been so far.

The views are beautiful and comforting to know that there are a lot of other travelers out here. The snow is still in the mountains and it is turning very cold. I doubt if it's any higher that 45 degrees. It's very overcast and looks like its snowing in the peaks of the mountains. 11:05 am and here we sit on an up-hill grade going up the mountain waiting for that, (words can't describe) pilot car. It is so dusty that our white poodle has turned brown.

IT REALLY IS A WHITE TRUCK CAP

Try to imagine if you can a dusty, dirty trail winding up and around the cliffs and all you can see in front of you are 20 to 30 other RV's going at a top speed of 15 miles an hour. It's like "Westward Ho", all of us curious fools wanting to see what's on the other side of the mountain.

I wish you could see the road we're on now. It is nothing but mud and if we stop we've had it. We just came into Teslin, a small settlement of mostly native people. Gas is now 58.7 per liter and almost 5 liter to a gallon, so you figure it out! We are 108 miles from Whitehorse and it took us 5 hours to go 198 miles. I think we are becoming basket cases, as we laugh at the least little thing. I think we have come about 800 miles since we left Dawson Creek and 650 of them have been just terrible.

We arrived in Whitehorse along with everyone else. It seems everyone headed for the same shopping center (maybe it's the only shopping center). We needed to stock up for the next leg of the trip. It's raining and very cold; children are still in snow suits. Whitehorse has a population of 14,000 and is situated on the banks of the Yukon River. The S.S. KLONDIKE still remains at the edge of town and provides interesting tours of the old sternwheeler.

S.S.KLONDIKE

Whitehorse has a lot of history and you can easily spend several days there, but due to our tight schedule this trip did not allow us much time. The area here is surrounded by mountains with little growth, but mostly clay soil. The Yukon River is to our right.

6 pm and we are 10 miles from Haines Junction. It is raining so hard that we can't see 10 feet in front of us. We still have approximately 1000 miles to Homer, Alaska, and final destination for this trip. We are in mountains that we saw a day or two back. These rock mountains are all between 10,000 to 12,000 feet tall and covered with snow. I wonder who ever named this a "highway". We are now pushing our way through mud. I am trying to be a good sport about this but it's difficult. I'm freezing; I'm dusty and dirty, tired and homesick. To think I could have gone to Europe, twice, for what this trip costs. Jerry just cheered me up by getting my flowers for the day; again they are lavender but a different variety.

We are traveling along the shores of Kluane Lake, the largest lake in the Yukon. The lake is more than 50 miles long and from the visibility we have its very beautiful.

Stopped at a mountain wilderness lodge and met a couple from Washington who now live in Anchorage. The woman is also a nurse who works in a burn unit. We really enjoyed their company and spent hours eating and drinking and just winding down. We spent the night parked against the repair garage, plugged in to their electric and had our little heater going all night to keep warm. We woke up to 30 degree weather, went in and took a shower at a cost of $2.50 per shower, and then went to the lodge for toast and coffee $6.00.

Started down the rough trail again. We came 472 miles yesterday and it took us 12 hours to do it. It is cloudy again, but sun poking through in places. It is so strange to see the peaks of the mountains and the clouds lower than the peaks.

You wouldn't believe the "road" we just came through; a trail of 6" mud. I don't know how we made it. The views are beautiful and it's almost like you were alone on a forbidden planet. When you go for miles and miles and see no signs of life, it gives you a strange feeling. We gained another hour and now at 11:45 am finally cross into Alaska. Once through customs we started out on a smooth blacktop (we'll see how long this lasts). No, I'm not optimistic at this point. Something new has been added since we came back into the US; guard rails! You won't believe it but we just got another chip in our windshield and we are on blacktop.

Just finishing cooking bacon, eggs, toast and coffee at a rest area, I tried to charge Jerry $14.60 but he wouldn't pay. Oh yes I forgot to mention that the Alaska border is clear out in the middle of no where, nothing there but the customs building.

It really is getting warmer, and so hard to believe that just a hundred or so miles back it was in the 30's. Stopped for gas and it was $163.9 per gallon and we thought it was high back on Pine Island.

We are now traveling south on the Glenn Highway towards Anchorage. The sun is bright and we are surrounded by beautiful mountains. The road is fair (spoke to soon we've been stopped for 20 minutes waiting for a pilot car). I've changed to shorts again. We meet a lot of interesting people when we stop to wait; we swap stories of the terrible roads and hear of all the people who are checking into selling their rigs and flying or taking the ferry back to Seattle from Haines. 6:10 pm and we are stopped at construction site again waiting for pilot car! Such fun! It's getting cloudy and we can't leave our windows down for the mosquitoes are awful. It's getting cooler and to the south there is a lot of snow in the mountains. We stopped for gas at Glennallen; 187 miles from Anchorage. We stopped at a mountain lodge for a hamburg and it was as big as a salad plate and really good. Now we are going to drive for a couple of hours to shake it down. Sun is really high yet.

June 30th, camped by a rushing creek last night, it was very soothing for a good nights sleep. We woke up at 3 am and it was as light as could be, the sun was still shining when we went to bed at 11:30 pm. It's a beautiful, crisp, sunny day and the clouds are nestled in the mountains.

Today we'll stay in Anchorage; do laundry, stock up and get a motel. Then tomorrow we will see our friends, Bud and Jackie. Now we are on a patched up black top and we've gone by several glacier areas. We went 390 miles yesterday. We came upon the Matanuska Glacier and what a spectacular sight. We are heading to Palmer and it is famous for its huge vegetables grown in the Matanuska Valley. This is a beautiful area but, the road consists of switch backs and we are driving high above the river. We are 15 days out and we've come 6009 miles. We stopped in Palmer for coffee and donuts and this time it was only $2.15.

Guess what? We are on a freeway; yes an honest to goodness freeway. Civilization sure does look good. Even though it has been a long, and at times unbearable journey, it sure is worth it. We can see Anchorage off in the distance and get this; the first sign we see is "Warning Moose Crossing" posted at the city limits. Anchorage is a very large city with a population of 240,000. Gas is 99.5 cents/gal. We pass an airport for small planes located within the city boundaries. Locals use them like we use cars to get around. Traffic is very heavy and reminds us of how much we prefer the wilderness.

Washed Lizzy, got groceries and now are headed to the south end of Anchorage. Words can't describe how beautiful this area is. Across the bay from Anchorage are the largest mountains yet and they are covered with snow from the base to the top. We were told that they are part of the Alaska Range.

We are traveling along the Cook Inlet where tides can vary 15 to 30 feet. We saw a moose standing way out where the tide had gone down and hoped he doesn't get stuck. We drove on to Cooper's Landing and found a place to camp right on the Kenai River. We did laundry and cooked supper outside. Took showers and then took a lot of pictures of the sun at 10:30 at night!

July 1; drove 245 miles yesterday and woke up to rain and fog. We set out for Homer at 10:30 am and have 120 miles to go. It continued to rain and in general be lousy. It will be great to see Bud and Jackie again and to not have to be on the road every day. We are looking forward to the fishing. Finally arrived in Homer and so good to see Bud and Jackie; so good to see familiar faces. We spent hours catching up and went on a sight seeing trip of the area that Bud so loves. It continued to rain and couldn't catch a glimpse of the mountains that surround us. We went down to the "Spit"; that's a piece of land that jets out in Kachemak Bay and is approximately 5 miles long and only a few hundred feet wide and this is where all the activity is. We went to the Salty Dog, a pub, with saw dust floors and everyone gathers there, tourists as well as locals. The Spit also is home to all the fishing activity, including a large boat harbor, several canneries, and a lot of fishing charters. It has numerous eating places and the usual tourist shops.

The most unique area is the "Fishing Hole". It is a man made pond dug out to let the waters of Kachemak Bay run in and out with the tides. At any given day during the season; there are numerous fisherman and onlookers hoping to either

26

catch or view the elusive salmon. The harbor is always full of the big commercial vessels and also pleasure crafts. The docks float up and down on poles as the tides vary so much.

RED, BUD AND JACKIE AT THE SPIT BOAT HARBOR

Bud and Jackie live in their 5th wheel trailer which is parked on their friend's property. There are also other people here in their trailers. We will park here during our time in Homer. The area is high on a hill with woods surrounding and is about 5 miles from Homer. There is big black lab and rabbits running all over. Mandy is taking this all in (she has never seen a rabbit before). Everyone is so friendly and we will find out what this area is all about.

July 2, had to have the heater on last night. Turned our little TV on and had good reception on 4 channels. We went to Jackie's for breakfast. Still overcast with poor visibility. We went into town and bought fishing license for the two of us; $40.00 for 14 days. We leave tomorrow or the next day on Bud's nephew's commercial boat and Jackie has been preparing me for what to expect. We came back to camp and ate smoked red salmon that they had done themselves; and so good! We turned in early; it's easy to sleep because it's so cold.

July 3rd went down to the boat and helped with the unloading process of a catch of salmon and prepared to leave on a day's fishing journey. We went out about 5 miles to set crab traps and I was able to do a lot of picture taking around Kachemak Bay. We even caught sight of a grey whale. We went to the little Homer airport to pick up the skipper's wife who flew in from Anchorage. Nine of us from camp went out to dinner, we stopped at a plain looking place; went in and sat down and the waitress brought the menus. We all turned a little green and for a second no one said a thing. Someone said "these prices are a little high, aren't they? Bud said "whose idea was this?" Someone mentioned should we get up and leave? And about that time we did just that. The prices were out of sight, hamburg was $7.50 and entrees started at $12.95. We went to another place and waited for over an hour, but cheaper and good food.

July 4th, we packed up early for a day of fishing for halibut with a crew of nine. We drove down to the Spit and loaded all the gear onboard. We are going to eat breakfast enroute. We set out and it was quite choppy and got worse the further out we went. I had eaten 2 donuts and when we stopped to start fishing I got sicker by the minute and spent my whole day between the head and the bunk. I don't think I've ever been so sick. Tomorrow I'll be sure to take something before I go out. We finally had to come in because it was so rough and we'll leave early tomorrow.

Came back to camp and the highlight of the 4th of July was when they threw firecrackers at the outhouse with Jerry inside. (He was a good sport about it).

July 5th and we went out in the boat again, this time I took some sea sick pills and did fine, but still very rough in Cook Inlet so we stayed in Kachemak Bay. The commercial fishermen here are on strike against the canneries and so most are staying in the harbor. We went for shrimp, very interesting; they put a long funnel shaped net in the water and drag it on the bottom in about 90 feet of water and then pull it in and take out the shrimp, fish, crab and what ever else is in the net. They throw anything back that is not in season. An abundant catch of shrimp was had by all at camp (after two hours of cleaning). Bud fixed the crab as we cleaned shrimp and we ate warm fresh snow crab. Turned in early, we have to start canning salmon and halibut tomorrow.

DAY OF FISHING WITH BUD

RED AND HIS CATCH OF SNOW CRAB

July 6th, canning day. We cut up and canned 36 jars of red salmon and halibut, quite an experience. Canning took a big part of the day and then we went into town for odds and ends. Jackie and Bud took us by their hospital and a look at other parts of town we had not seen yet. Came back and had steamed shrimp, scalloped potatoes, baked beans, coleslaw, garlic bread, pumpkin pie and upside down pineapple cake; so you see we are really on a diet! We went to bed early; you sure get tired here because all they do is work. Cook Inlet is still very rough so doubt if we'll get out any more or not.

July 7th is a beautiful day. Sunny and about 55 degrees. Today we are going to the local museum, do laundry and pick up 3 rolls of pictures. I can hardly wait to see them to find out if I'm doing everything right. Waters are extremely rough so we can't even go clam digging because you need to get in a small boat and go across open water to the other side of the bay.

Today I want to do more picture taking. If water is still rough we may leave here on Monday and head towards Fairbanks. My last pictures turned out great. Jackie and I peeled little baby shrimp till we were sick of them. We had deep fried salmon steaks and a shrimp salad for supper. It's going to be hard to go back to "regular food". The museum was really interesting, all kinds of stuffed animals and an in-depth history of Homer and Alaska in general.

Our days are so full we fall into bed and sleep like babies. Had to take Mandy to the local vet, she has been so hyper with all the changes in her regular routine and the vet had to put her on tranquilizers. It was funny to watch her after she had just one pill, she acted like a little drunk, I'll cut her down to ½ tab and see what that does for her.

July 8th and temperature is 50 degrees and rain, just an awful day and did nothing more than get up and have breakfast, visited with Bud and Jackie and came back to camper and watched TV. We are taking Bud and Jackie out to dinner later and will pack up and leave tomorrow. Seas are still very rough and most ships are in port. Coast Guard has been called out for a rescue. We have a lot of things we want to do yet and will head towards Fairbanks tomorrow. Still have 7 days left on our fishing license and will fish in the streams along the way.

July 9th and we left Bud and Jackie at 10 am. We had quite a morning. Bud has all sorts of CB Radios and VHF marine radios which they monitor continually because of their family and friends out in boats. This am they heard of a 40 foot charter boat (with passengers) sinking just off the bluff from them. We walked to the bluff and sure enough there it was. It was 1 to 2 miles off shore and other boats were already there, seas were very rough and the bow was listing. Coast Guard planes and choppers came and when we left they were dropping a pump and a larger ship had a line to the sinking one. All the passengers were off and safe.

Being with Bud and Jackie was quite an experience and we learned a lot about fishing and the way of life here. It's strictly a fishing village, filled with tourists from all over the world. It is also a Mecca for college kids that come here by the hundreds and camp out on the beach and work in the canneries or on charter boats. If they have the experience there is commercial fishing possibilities. The money is good and they have a great summer too!

We continued our journey towards Anchorage and stopped at Portage Glacier that is approximately 40 miles south of Anchorage. It is a must on the tourist schedule. The glacier is large and descends within ones grasp. The ice is a beautiful blue and to think it has been here for centuries.

We left the glacier and went a bit further for a try "gold panning" and no luck. The area was an original old mine with original buildings. Jerry found one tiny flake and we decided we would be better at working for a living; but it was fun and we can say we went gold mining in Alaska.

RED LOOKING FOR GOLD

31

We stayed in a motel last night in the town of Wasilla, which is 40 miles north of Anchorage. You wouldn't believe this area! Everything is new and the whole area is booming. We asked why. We were told that there was talk of shifting the capital of Alaska to this area from Juneau but it didn't materialize. Still is growing in leaps and bounds. The wages in this area are, truck drivers $18 to $20 an hour, teachers $32,000 to $40,000 a year, Director of Nursing $58,000 a year and nurses $15 to $19 an hour. Sure is a place for young people who want to work hard, make good money and live in a beautiful land. Land is really high, but really no more than what you pay in Florida for comparable land that is in demand. Houses are mostly of cedar or redwood nestled in pines. Its noon now and we are headed north on Highway 3 towards the Denali National Park. Another bad day; raining and heavy cloud cover (we have had our share of bad weather). We can't even see the mountains.

We are close to Denali but unable to catch a glimpse. We are 22 miles from the park entrance. Just had coffee in Cantwell, town has no taxes of any kind, also has no electricity. Everyone has their own generator. There is no city water, sewer, or lights. This area is different and very beautiful; it's almost as if you were traveling on the surface of a different planet with only the highway and the traffic to remind you of where you are. We have traveled 7000 miles to see the big mountain and chances are we won't. Only 40% of the people ever see it.

We went to the visitor center and every campsite if full. We'll have to be at the park entrance at least by 5 am tomorrow to see if we can get a site. You only can drive in the park just a few miles if you don't have a permit and then you can only drive the distance that it takes to get to your site. There are school buses that go in and out of the park all day. The entire trip is 85 miles one way. They don't want you driving because of the protection of the animals. We are about 1 ½ miles from the entrance, parked along side of the McKinley River and every so often we see rafts filled with 6 to 8 people floating by. It looked like fun, but Jerry said the water was too cold for him.

July 11th and what a day we had. We set the alarm for 4 am; got up and drove to park entrance and already there were at least 10 people standing in line at the office to sign up for a camp site or an early bus. I made coffee and Jerry went and stood in line from 4:20 am to 5:30 am when the park office opened. There were at least 200 people in line then. It was a beautiful morning; light as could be and sunny too!

RED IN LINE WITH HIS TWO CUPS OF COFFEE TO KEEP WARM

We were about 12<sup>th</sup> in line and we were able to get the campground we wanted 29 miles into the park, which meant we could drive that far and the rest of the trip we would have to catch one of the many school buses that make their rounds.

Started into the park and 1 mile in was the Park Hotel; very unique. The hotel rooms are Pullman cars from the Alaskan Railroad and they are grouped around a building which not only has a dining room and lounge, but also serves as the train depot for the link between Fairbanks and Anchorage. Passengers can get off here and hop on a shuttle bus (school bus) to the end of the park. We stopped for breakfast and then continued on with our journey and when we reached the 8 mile point we sighted the majestic Mt. McKinley also known as "Denali". What a sight and this was at 7 am and we were very lucky to be among the few that do catch a glimpse. The mountain is enormous and covered with snow from base to top. The clouds were already moving in and it wasn't long till she was no longer visible. We were still some 75 miles away from the end of the park and even then at the closest point from the road you are still some 25 miles from the base. I took many pictures and hope they turn out and show justice to the awesome sight.

The mountains for the first 20 miles are tundra covered and very little snow, just very green with peaks of rock, quite a contrast to Mt. McKinley which is entirely covered with snow. We arrived at our camp site at 8:30 am and we had our pick of sites. We promptly parked and went back to bed. Got up and caught the 12:15 bus.

This time we had a woman driver and she was very nice in giving all the passengers information. We headed into the park and at first the landscape was much like our campground; small spruce tree's, lots of willow and tundra. The mountains looked like pastures and you could spot things far off. Our first sighting was two golden eagles, followed shortly by doll sheep. The scenery then changed to shear cliffs of rock with tundra below and guess who was on the cliff side of the bus? Us! With real sharp switch backs, narrow gravel road with no guard rails and I swear they rode right on the edge. At points the driver made mention that the cliffs were 3000 feet straight down and if that wasn't enough you should have seen how bad it was to meet another bus. In spite of the fear; I wish everyone could see this park, but if you don't like heights, forget it!

We saw several caribou in different sightings and more sheep. Jerry was getting disappointed at not seeing any bull moose or bear. We arrived at Eielson's headquarters, which is 65 miles into the park and it was 3:15 pm, so it had taken us 3 hours to go 35 miles. We decided not to go the additional 20 miles as clouds had come in over the mountain and it didn't look like we would sight her again. We signed up for a return bus and went out on the observation deck and there about 200 yards out we sight our first grizzly of medium size sleeping on the hill side. After a while it got up and started in our direction stopping to feed at times. We walked down about 50 to 60 yards on a bluff to get a closer look. It was bigger than we first thought; very light brown, almost blonde in color. I took pictures but it was still far off. Jerry was finally happy and I was thrilled to death.

We boarded a different bus for the return trip, driven by a young man and from the minute we took off I knew I wasn't going to like his driving. He took the curves like he was driving in the Indy 500. We came upon three more grizzly bears, all in single sightings. We were told that only the female and her cubs travel as a group. The rest of the time the bears will be traveling alone unless they are mating.

He told us of a male bear who attacked a female and her two cubs. The males will kill the cubs to bring the female into season. This particular male took a swipe at one of the cubs breaking it's back and the mother bear came after the male and after about 2 hours of fighting the male killed the female and buried her; returning to feed on the carcass at intervals. The park rangers are reluctant to interfere with the animals here and allow nature to take its course, but did evaluate if the cub could be saved if they took it out. They could not save it and even though it was a cub they were concerned that people might chance upon it and someone would get hurt so they had to put it down. The other cub was an orphan, but had not been sighted.

Made it back to camp very tired. We checked again on the climbing permit and no additional ones are being offered in this area (you have to apply 2 to 3 months ahead). Our night came to a close with a thunderstorm and heavy rain. This has been quite a day, one we will never forget.

July 12th and we woke up to a sunny, clear and cold morning. We left camp at 8:30 and started our 30 miles out of the park. We sighted the majestic mountain again and were able to see her for quite a few miles; we really feel fortunate in being able to see it not once, but twice. We met some people yesterday who had been here 5 years ago and didn't see it and had not seen it this time either. We will head for Fairbanks this morning. Spotted a big moose along the highway and now we are 50 miles from Fairbanks traveling through a valley with views of the mountains in the distance. We've been on fair roads except for construction areas. When we arrived in Fairbanks it was 77 degrees, what a change from the cold of last night. Fairbanks is a town of old history and new development. We didn't get much time there due to our tight schedule, but maybe will get here again sometime. We passed by the settlement of the North Pole; famous for answering the mail of the kids around the world. We continued our journey to Tok, which is a very small settlement which provides a good stopping off place to get supplies, gas, do laundry, camp and head up the Glen highway to Anchorage or continue the Alcan Highway to the US border.

It has been raining most of the day. It's hard to leave Alaska, knowing I'll probably never get the opportunity to return. This country gets in your blood and words can't explain why it lures you back. We stopped at a little café, lodge, gas station, grocery store and repair shop. All of these remote facilities are like this. There is no zoning, so you can expect most anything.

Traveling the same route back, but it looks different even though we have been here before. The mountains change with every cloud. At times it is breath taking. We made it through Friday the 13th unless something happens in the next hour, and it may very well do just that.

Jerry out did himself in his choice of parking for the night. We are about 15 miles west of Whitehorse and pulled down by a creek, backed into the woods and we have a garbage pile at our back door. By the looks of things a bear has rummaged through it all! And this is where Jerry hopes to see his bear, right by the camper. I don't know about him, but Mandy and I are not setting foot outside. Let you know how it works out.

July 14th, woke up to a beautiful sunny morning and no bear! Largest critter was a chipmunk. Headed into Whitehorse and going to stock up and head down the Cassiar Highway. Its 458 miles back to Prince Rupert and mostly on gravel roads (couldn't be any worse than the rest of the trip). You can always tell when you are getting close to town, I mentioned before that there is no zoning and there is usually what I call junk all over; only it isn't junk, its things that you may need in the future. Remember, here you are not around the corner from the local Wal-Mart.

Turned south on the Cassiar Highway and so far a real nice gravel road. Very hilly and densely populated with spruce trees. Facilities are few and far between and the next one is at 122 km. 9 pm and we've traveled about 80 miles, this road is unlike the Alaskan Highway. The road winds around and through the mountains at the base and valleys and so far not much cliff driving. The mountains are the Cassiar Range, very high and snow covered. There is still mining for gold going on in places. There are deserted log cabins and we passed a cemetery with white wooden crosses all the same size. The dwellings we did see seem to be occupied by natives. We're going on for another 60 miles and shut down for the night.

July 15th, parked behind a combined café, gas station, grocery store and repair shop. We went to a café in the morning for coffee. The building was made out of massive logs and had a wonderful home atmosphere. They told us where to buy a Canada fishing license and we went to see the clerk. You should see this place; this guy has several old trailers put together and, can and will sell, barter or trade anything. He sells insurance, fishing licenses, junk, second hand things, furs, fish, bait and information. He told us about a 70 mile trail into the most beautiful country

36

in British Columbia. He said we could catch salmon, trout and he would buy any that we didn't want. He further stated that at the end of the road was a native settlement of about 300 people living like they did back in the gold rush days, so we decided to take the side trip.

Right now we're at a beautiful creek and Jerry is fishing, sun is out bright and this is really virgin country. We heard this morning that the Alaskan Highway was closed at Muncho Lake, between Watson Lake and Fort Nelson, due to flooding.

The native village is called Telegraph Creek and we continue to wind our way on this little road and the scenery is breathtaking; wild roses along the road edges, tall pines, and wild horses every so often. We are now at the 37th mile into the canyon, passed by some native women picking wild strawberries along the road edges. We are descending now on a 10% grade to the valley below. Thousands of years ago a volcano erupted leaving a lava bed below us. We are now on a switch back of sheer cliffs and a one lane bridge that crosses a beautiful river below. Just came around a bend and in the mountain sides were hundreds of small holes, and all of a sudden hundreds of bats flew out at us, we quickly rolled up the windows and watched from the comfort of our closed up vehicle.

The area continues to be switchbacks with views so beautiful that it's hard to believe even when were right here. Came across some natives fishing, they were not very friendly. Drove on through some of the most terrifying cliffs you can imagine, some of which it seemed like a thousand foot drop to river below. Passed by an area high above us with white fence around white crosses, we thought it might be an Indian Cemetery, we didn't see any trail so I don't know how they got up there.

This area is really primitive and we have just a few more miles before we get to the village. We were somewhat surprised when the first buildings we saw were fairly new structures; ranch style modular homes, plain but modern. The people here are subsidized by the government. We descended even further into the canyon to the river. We came to the end of the road to Stikine Riversong Café and Lodge which was formerly the old Hudson Bay Store in the early 1900's. The café was run by white people; who served very good food. We had chili and homemade bread and coffee, cost $12.00. Met a girl there who was from California who was traveling with a young man from Australia and they were traveling around the world, mostly in a kayak, very interesting to talk with them.

The buildings in the village were very old; I'd say the village consisted of nothing more than a grouping of shacks built at different levels in the slope of the mountain. We started our climb out of the canyon, stopping every so often to look at the gorges below. Came back to an area where the natives had been fishing and went up stream from them to try our luck, difference was they could net them and we couldn't. Several big king salmon were caught by other people but none by us. At times the younger natives would walk around us and it was a little testing of the nerves. They wouldn't say anything, just look at you and even when we said "Hi", they wouldn't respond. We tried fishing for a couple of hours and it was getting late so started back out. We still had those cliffs and switchbacks ahead and it was 8:30 pm already. To give you an idea of what we're driving on, at one point we were about 400 feet above 2 rivers and we were on a natural bridge of rock about 30 feet wide with a steep drop to the river.

We traveled on and it got dark, came around a sharp bend and there were 5 horses in the road. We were hoping to see one of the huge grizzlies that the man had told us about (up to 11 feet high when standing), but probably would have died if we had. We were also told of the large black wolf population; but didn't see any of those either. We got back to where we had camped the night before and I sure was glad to see civilization again. It took us over 3 hours to go 50 miles. I was so tired and nerved up that it was easy to imagine being scalped by an Indian or attacked by bats, wolves or grizzlies.

It rained hard most of the night and I was very glad we had not stayed back there as the roads are all clay.

July 16th woke up at 6:45 to another cloudy day, went to café for coffee and toast and met the couple we had met yesterday in the canyon. Started south again and will try our luck at fishing along the way. We dropped down into a lush valley with mountains all around, many water falls and lush vegetation with trees that look like redwood. Road is muddy and all vehicles look the same color. Lizzy will get a bath once we get to civilization. The snow is at such low elevations you can walk to it. You should see the bridges on this route; all single lane, wooden and creaky.

Stopped for nature break, checked truck and found both headlights were full of holes and not working. We do have spares but will not drive at night till we get off the gravel. Stopped at a creek to try fishing; no fish but you sure can do a lot with creek water, i.e. washed dishes, brushed teeth, washed face, hands and feet (not warm enough for other parts), washed lizzy, and cooled hard boiled eggs.

DO ALL WITH COLD NATURAL RUNNING WATER

Continued our journey towards Bear Glacier, which is just before you come to Stewart, British Columbia which is on the Alaska/Canada border. Stewart lies at the head of a 90 mile canal which leads to the Gulf of Alaska. We are stopped at the famous one stop shopping, gas, motel and food places and headed for Stewart after leaving the awesome Bear Glacier. We are on beautiful new asphalt, mountains are 14,000 to 16,000 feet and the highway is built at the base. Stewart is a small village and one has to wonder what these people do for a living 70 miles back in here. The US border is here and we entered into Hyder, Alaska. This town is small too and very primitive with dirt streets and very few facilities. Both of these towns are a stones throw from each other. We discovered that Hyder has 3 bars and a population of 90. We went into one bar that was really different. The bartender had a baby in his arms while waiting on customers and there were wall to wall kids under age 5. I guess you do what you have to do to make a living!

BEAR GLACIER

THE TOWN OF HYDER, ALASKA

Saw a pair of golden eagles feeding on salmon and we sure did see the salmon; the creeks and rivers were full of them. We tried our luck at fishing but no luck. I decided to fix dinner while Jerry was fishing and all of a sudden he said "bear,

bear" and sure enough there was a black bear 200 feet away on the opposite shore coming our way and Jerry decided that he would leave the fish for the bear. We drove on down and there we sighted a grizzly bear (blonde in color). What a day, we fixed one of our lights and will drive on for a while and drove on till after dark (no midnight sun in this area at this time of year) we camped by a stream and woke up to a beautiful day. We've been camping every day now for 8 days and need to get a motel to get humanized.

July 17th, forgot to mention that last night we could hear the howls of wolves in the distance. We will be heading for Prince George and back to the "real world", we will never forget all the experiences we've had and we really have done some high adventure experiences. We traveled over 12,000 miles on this trip and as you will read in our next chapters; every trip gets better. We gain more knowledge and even become "true fisherman". Even the roads get better in the years ahead and one thing to remember "You may leave Alaska, but Alaska will never leave you ".

# FIVE YEARS LATER

It's been five long years of waiting to return to Alaska and the day has arrived. We leave this year driving a 1979 van that has been converted to make us as comfortable as possible. We had lunch with friends, John and Donna, and left on May 11, 1989.

This year we hope to take it slower and really see some of the areas that we only briefly visited before. We are allowing three months this time, and I will also work at the hospital in Homer a few shifts a week. We have been eager to return to Alaska since the last trip.

TRANSPORTATION TO/FROM ALASKA IN 1989

When we are in Homer we will be living in Bud and Jackie's 5th wheel as they are now in their mobile home on Bud's nephew's property and we will be right next to them.

We departed St. James City, Florida and headed north on Interstate 75, the temperature was 72 degrees, quite cool for May in Florida. Our route will take us further northwest this year and we will enter Canada through Washington State.

May 13, spent the night in rest area on US 70 just west of St. Louis, Missouri. The temperature got down to 42 degrees. This morning however it is beautiful, sunny and about 65 already. We ate breakfast outside listening to the birds and hearing the wind whistle through the new leaves on the trees. It is just breaking spring here and everything looks so fresh and green.

We left with a new book given to us by a Deb, a nurse at work. *Cashing in on the American Dream*, states that you can live pretty well on $50.00 a day. So far we aren't making it! I guess I'd better read the book again. Jerry is more than ever convinced this being "foot loose and fancy free" is the only way to go.

Mother's Day May 14, spent the night at Sundowner's Campground in the middle of a prairie, wind died down and we cooked outside. Took showers and felt 100% better and spent the rest of the night watching TV.

We made more preparation for this trip by allowing more time. We also invested in a video camera (I'll probably bore everyone to death). We left the campground at 9:30 and a very cloudy day. Everything here is burning up; fields all have a grey/brown cast and ones thoughts are about the people who see their whole life going down the tube with a drought such as this. We should see snow covered mountains today, I just hope the snow is only on the mountains.

Drove till 12:45 am, sure had one big shock; we expected to see snow in the distance but not to drive in it. We came through a blinding snow fog with everything covered with fresh snow. It actually was beautiful, at least from inside the van. We also came upon our first accident, a semi had hit a car and it looked like it exploded on impact. The vehicle was in pieces and the passengers (dead or alive) had already been removed and I was relieved of that. We also spotted our first antelope. We developed a small leak in one of our hoses, but Jerry managed to fix it.

Sun is out and it's 32 degrees, cold but refreshing. We have about 100 miles before we get to Utah. We used the comforter last night to keep warm. Mandy is not quite sure what to think about the changes in temperature.

Treated ourselves to modern luxuries last night; a Best Western Hotel complete with bathtub and color TV. We really were looking for a campground, but their idea of camping on this stretch of road at least is to park your vehicle in a field with a map to the outhouse! We are on the road again, on Highway 26, heading west to Bend, Oregon. For a while last night it looked like we were already in Alaska!

There were remote areas for miles winding through several different types of mountains; first with only sage brush for cover and then into dark, thick forests with tall pine trees. We finally came onto the town of John Day. The town is rich with Indian history named after the Indian, John Day. Life back in these mountains by our standards is very primitive and lacking, but by their standards very rich I'm sure or at best just existing. Soon we will see our son and his wife and also our two grand daughters, all of whom we haven't seen for 3 years.

May 17, and back on road again, heading for Portland, Oregon. We spent the day with our son and family. They live in a beautiful area and plan on building soon. They had to work today so we had breakfast and bid our good byes, not knowing when the next time to see each other would be. The girls had really grown and soon they will be out of school for the summer. We're heading for Portland and it is real hazy, but yesterday we did manage to get clear bright pictures of Mount Hood and today you can hardly see the mountains.

It is now 4:00 pm and we are in British Columbia, we've come through a 50 mile canyon that is to beautiful for words. We've driven the last two days through rain and cold and we called Carla, (our daughter), in Grand Rapids, Michigan and it was 81 degrees. Its 30 degrees where we were. We spent the night in a KOA campground in Bellingham, Washington and it was the cleanest one we had ever stayed in. We did the laundry, first time since leaving home. We have been out now for 7 days and Jerry isn't feeling too well, started with some abdominal pain, he has been watching his diet carefully so I'm concerned as to what is going on. He has Ulcerative Colitis and it flares up often.

As the day progressed he felt a little better. We drove till 11 pm and stopped just west of Prince George on the Yellow Head Highway. We woke up to 30 degree weather, but at least it's not raining. We drove for 2 days in the rain and late yesterday afternoon drove through a snow storm again. So now we're on the road again and can see the coastal mountains off in the distance, capped with snow. They are the highest ones of our trip so far. Sun is out, very windy and temperature is about 35 degrees. Each time we let Mandy out she looks at us as if to say "what are we doing here?"

May 20, and we are now on the Alaskan Highway (loose term for trail), just saw another car that went over the mountain. We drove the Cassiar Highway yesterday and ran into yet another snow storm. Stayed at Deese Lake last night and started out at 8 am. It's very cold, lake is still frozen over. We are now headed for Whitehorse and they are expecting a snow storm too. So hard telling what we're in for. Saw a black bear, snowshoe rabbit, big horn sheep and porcupine.

Stopped at campground in Whitehorse, was going to stay at motel, but they wanted $85.00 per night for a "flea bitten room"; no thanks we'll stay in the van. We do have a lot of dust on everything. It's fairly warm here; they didn't get the snow that was forecast. Jerry is just coming back from the shower (looks better) and now it's my turn.

Sun is still high at 10 pm and we've had our camp supper and will relax for the night. Tomorrow we head for the Alaska border, still some 300 miles of dust away. Jerry is feeling better, but we are really tired. We have "van lag" and right now it sure is nice to be setting still.

THE ALASKA BORDER

We entered the border to Alaska and on to Tok, Alaska, where we stayed at another campground, had quite a day. It was a beautiful one, with sun out all day and we took spectacular views of Kluane Lake (in the Yukon), roads were very rough and I'd hate to see them in another couple of weeks. After the frost works out of the ground, they will be pure mud. We came through US Customs around 5 pm. It's very windy now and very cold and we are at the base of the St. Elias Mountains which are covered with snow. We're about two weeks early and most facilities are closed yet.

We called Bud and Jackie and plan on meeting them in Anchorage on the 23rd. We're going to see some of the town, go out to Bud and Jackie's favorite Chinese restaurant and then the next day go for supplies before heading to Homer. We'll come back to Anchorage in about 6 weeks for more supplies (to expensive and scarce in Homer).

Arrived in Anchorage last night and treated ourselves to a Holiday Inn; sure felt good! Left at 10 am to wash the van, do some laundry and get breakfast. Met Bud and Jackie at 1:30 and spent the evening visiting and had a fabulous dinner. We stayed at Bud's nephew's house high up in the mountains overlooking Anchorage.

May 24th, met Bud and Jackie for lunch and then went to Costco's for supplies. Jerry went "hog wild" there. What a place. We're hoping that SAM'S that is being built in Ft. Myer's, Florida will be like this store. You can buy anything for a lot less.

The next morning we left for Homer. The 240 mile trip took us 5½ hours. We arrived at their new location (different from that of 1984). They are located on a bluff overlooking Kachemak Bay with a beautiful a view of the Glaciers. The property belongs to Bud's nephew and it has the largest spruce trees I've ever seen. We proceeded to move into the 5th wheel that will be our home while we're in Homer. Around the 5th wheel are the biggest moose tracks we've seen and last week a black bear was in camp, so we'll be a little careful. At the camp there is Bud and Jackie's mobile and his nephew's mobile, plus several semi trailers which store all the gear needed to catch, freeze and process fish. We spent our first night in our "new home", snug as a bug in a rug.

May 26th, got up to a cold morning, 30 something and went into the little town here (about 2 miles from here) and bought fishing licenses for the both of us. Total $72.00 each... We better get fishing! Went out on the Spit to get the water barrels filled, and then bring back to camp to put in to a big cistern. Water is extremely expensive to drill for. On the bluff here you would have to go 200 to 300 feet and then maybe not even hit water. We saw 9 eagles sitting on the beach on the Spit and one large moose on the way back to camp and guess what? No camera.

THE 5<sup>th</sup> WHEEL   ~   OUR HOME FOR THE SUMMER

We did the laundry, took on some additional groceries (very, very expensive to buy here). Jackie made stew and homemade biscuits; so good! Tomorrow we go back north about 75 miles to go "hooligan fishing" on the Kenai River. Today it is very cold and raining on and off, so the weather will be the deciding factor. I finally received my Alaska nursing license, so will get serious about doing a couple of days a week soon. Jerry hooked up the TV and micro wave oven, so now we're back to the luxuries of life.

We weren't able to go fishing, due to the rain and cold. Instead we viewed the tapes of our trip and just rested, hoping for a better day tomorrow. Bud gave us our mail and delighted to hear from people back home. I really do miss the routine of work and especially the people who are more a part of your life that you think. Jerry is feeling better now and hopes he continues that way.

Still miserable weather and we're staying inside. Jerry and Bud went down to the Spit and I made supper for everyone.

May 29<sup>th</sup> Memorial Day. It's still rotten weather with less rain, but very overcast. Going to friend's house for dinner and tomorrow I'll go to the hospital and check things out. Tomorrow we leave to try hooligan fishing once again, rain or shine, but it is scheduled to be better.

Went to the hospital today and was really impressed at the facility and the very friendly staff. I had to stand my ground about not working full time and agreed to no more than 3 days a week. Tomorrow I have my lab, x-rays and even a rubella titer test (they had a recent measles outbreak). I start 2 weeks of orientation on Monday and then will work 3 to 11 which is their busiest shift. The median age here is 28. They have a lot of boating related accidents and they are building a huge dam at Bradley Lake which is at the head of Kachemak Bay, and they have had their fair amount of trauma accidents related with this project.

Today we finally went hooligan fishing and really had a ball filling two-5 gallon buckets. These fish are all about 10" long and you wade out in glacier mud and drag a net through the water. The fish are like our Michigan smelt. I met three Russian girls who were fishing alone. They were dressed in their colorful dresses (even while fishing), bright scarves, coats and boots. They were covered with mud. I found them very friendly after I initiated the conversation. They did speak broken English and the rest of the time spoke in Russian. They even allowed me to film them. As I sat there on the bank, my mind would wander and I felt as though I was the luckiest girl in the world to be able to experience all of this. If you can imagine sitting on the Kenai River, surrounded by mountains with 3 Russian girls right by you and across the meadow are 3 of the largest Caribou I've seen and to top it off you are looking at Mt. Redoubt (an active volcano) across Cook Inlet.

THE FISHING HOLE

June 1, and today we are going salmon fishing in the "fishing hole" on the Spit. We fished our hearts out and no luck, but we'll try again tomorrow. We actually got a little sun burned or maybe it is wind burnt. We are really comfortable in our 5th wheel and are enjoying every day to the fullest and have no problem sleeping.

Real cold and rainy today, tried to go salmon fishing but rained most of day. We did the laundry and drove out to the east bay area to get chemicals for the toilet in the 5th wheel. Stopped at a bakery and café, had coffee and each had a roll, cost $4.99; guess we won't be doing that very often. This quaint town is loaded with college kids. They're here for the summer to work in the local canneries or on the charter boats. It sure seems strange to be around so many young people. We got back to camp and just missed the chance to see Mamma Moose and her two babies; they had come into camp around Bud and Jackie's trailer and across the driveway and all we saw were the tracks. Bud said the babies were real small. May and June are when most calves are born and the moose have their calves close to people to be away from bears, wolves and other predators.

Mandy and I went for a walk and I let her sniff the moose tracks and she was ready to go hunting. We watch her real close, she is always on a leash, but even then we keep an eye on her. She herself is at risk from owls, eagles, and of course bears, and wolves. Tomorrow I go for my physical. South Peninsula Hospital in Homer is a small hospital that not only serves Homer, but also covers a wide area including several villages across the bay. The next closest hospital is Soldotna, and that is 70 miles away. Most of the critical cases get flown to Anchorage.

Went for my physical; everything ok. Came back to camp, raining off and on and still cold. We decided to move the 5th wheel to its permanent spot now that the gravel base is complete. We now have the bay and mountains on one side and the woods on the other, you can't possibly imagine the view we have. The one disadvantage is that now we're in the woods more and the mosquitoes are awful. Tomorrow we hope to go salmon fishing and this time catch one.

Today Tom Schroeder, a fish and game biologist, and good friend brought us two king salmon and one sockeye salmon, so Jerry got up and cleaned, staked and smoked fish while I did the routine cleaning in the 5th wheel. Later in the day we went fishing, Jerry finally got one on, really gave him a fight and in the end it was snagged and had to turn it loose. We came back to camp and we all had BBQ salmon steaks. We now have our own water hooked in direct and turned the hot water heater on and took showers. We are really civilized now!

Tomorrow I go to work and Jerry will be busy clearing brush and trimming trees around camp. Jackie wants a screen room built and Bud wants a pump house built to hold the 500 gallon water supply. We will work 3 days and play the other 4, not too bad.

Well today was D-Day—worked 7am to 3pm (well better explained) I was someone's shadow. The nurses here do everything and very skilled at what they do. The ER has beautiful equipment and extremely clean. They are short staffed here like every where else, but I'm holding my ground and don't want to work any more than 3 days a week. Staff is very friendly and helpful.

June 7th and I have been working 3 to 11 (the weather has been beautiful), wouldn't you know it. We went fishing yesterday on the big commercial boat, owned by Bud's nephew. We had a great day, fairly calm seas, but cold. We left the harbor and went out for about one hour before dropping anchor. We fished for about 4 hours and Jerry caught a "huge" halibut that put up quite a fight.

RED SCRUBBING DOWN THE DECK

He also caught a smaller one and he was the only one to catch fish big enough to bring home. I didn't catch a thing. When we weighed the halibut back at camp, we realized why it gave such a fight; it weighed 72 pounds. Jerry sure was excited and I shot a lot of video. We sure were tired after a full day on the water. Tomorrow Jerry gets to clean his fish and then I get to can it. We sure are having the time of our life. We also managed to sight sea otters, sea lions and many eagles.

First shift in the ER tonight, started slow and ended with a bang! We worked a code for two hours on a 65 year old man who just refused to die, but also wasn't doing a good job of living, just enough to keep the code going. They are very aggressive here and really good! I am really impressed at just how good the entire staff is. I finally made it home at 1:15 am.

This morning Mamma Moose and her babies came strolling up the drive and I managed to capture them on film. It is so exciting to see them.

MAMMA MOOSE AND HER BABIES

June 10th and work last night was normal and I sure do like it here. I got up at 7 am and canned 47 ½ pints of halibut. We discovered that we have our own "Moose Club" here and I don't mean a lodge. Today Mandy started growling and I looked out the trailer door and there stood a moose about 40 feet from me. First I put Mandy in the bathroom and then grabbed the camera, opened the door and started filming. It stayed close to camp for about an hour, but when I got a little to close it let me know by raising the hair on the back of his or her neck; really exciting !

THE HAIR RAISING MOOSE

Tonight we are treating Bud and Jackie to dinner out. It's the first night out for a long time, we just don't have time and really like eating the fresh fish, crab and mussels. We are kept very busy with fishing, cleaning fish, processing fish or just visiting around camp. Jackie and Bud have some kind of respiratory problem and can't seem to shake it. Jerry is fine and so am I. It's raining here again and temperature is about 50 degrees. We sure have had awful weather lately.

Doug and Lil MacElroy (friends from Florida) called Bud and Jackie last night and are leaving for New York in a few days and then start from there for their long drive here. Sure will be good to see them. My schedule at work has changed a little, I'll be working every Thursday, Friday and Saturday, but that's ok I'll still have Sunday, Monday, Tuesday and Wednesday to play.

Today we had another encounter with the Bull Moose; he got a little to close and when we tried to chase him off he resisted and came towards us. He's approximately 2 years old and guess just a little testy. We canned another 16 jars of halibut and went down to the Spit to try our luck at salmon fishing again and again no luck.

We need to take both Bud and Jackie to the doctor tomorrow. Jackie has had these "flu like" symptoms for about 2 weeks and now Bud apparently has it too; so I'm glad they agreed to go.

June 12th; took Bud and Jackie to the doctor and ended up admitting Bud to the hospital He was wheezing quite a bit and not moving much air (Bud has emphysema), the doctor didn't think it had reached the point of pneumonia yet, and today both Jerry and I are starting with the same symptoms. We sure are tired of everyone being so sick, but everyone in town seems to have the same thing.

Visited Bud tonight and he seemed a little better and I feel better that he is in the hospital as he really doesn't have much reserve like all the rest of us.

June 13th and forget the fishing; it's raining again! I went with Jackie to visit Bud and he is feeling much better and no pneumonia. Jerry isn't feeling any better and slept all day.

June 15th we went for a drive to get out in the fresh air and caught a good view of Mt. Augustine; about 80 miles west of Homer, in the Cook Inlet. Mt. Augustine is an active volcano and further west is McNeil River and I hope to get over there this summer to film the large influx of bears feeding on the salmon. We stopped by the American Legion Post and talked with some interesting people and learned more history of this area. The sun was out bright today. Bud is doing ok but still in the hospital. Jackie, Jerry and I packaged all the rest of our fish and put it in the freezer. We had Jackie over for supper. Tomorrow I work 3 to 11 and sure hope I feel better.

June 18th and Bud finally got to come home, and today Jackie and I took our husbands to the American Legion for a Father's Day brunch. Then Jerry and I went exploring the area. Drove out to East End Road to the head of Kachemak Bay, or at

53

least we went as far as the road went and then had to turn around, but there was a trail that continued on to a Russian village. The road was terrible, with some area's just disappearing. We then drove up to the top of Sky Line Drive and the sight was the most beautiful I've ever seen in all of our travels. (We filmed it all and can't wait to share).

THE SPIT FROM SKYLINE DRIVE

Got back to camp and the hospital had called needing someone to work, I could work 7 days a week, but I'm standing firm and will only do 3 days per week.

June 19$^{th}$ and today Jerry is starting the project of building Bud a "smoke house", it's real tall and like the Indians used to build; fish are cut into strips and cold smoked and they call it squaw candy. Believe it or not; I laid out in the sun, I took a piece of foam and laid it in the pickup box where I was protected by the wind. It really got warm (different).

It is cooler today and real windy. Everyone here is feeling much better, so hope it stays that way. Jerry is working hard on the smoke house and soon we need to go get water and a few supplies. Later we went fishing and Jerry out-fished me again. He catches them and I am getting better with netting them. He caught 2 king salmon and tomorrow they will smoke them. Tomorrow the tide will really be low so we hope to go 30 to 40 miles north of here and dig for razor clams.

Bud still isn't doing to well, he has a good day and then a bad one; now he is having a problem with his feet swelling, and not a good sign and he goes back to the doctor tomorrow.

June 22nd, and Bud was admitted again; he isn't doing well at all and only able to walk about 12 feet before setting down to rest.

We went for clams today, down on the Spit. We had never done this and went out to the flats where the tide was out; dug up some clams and we were so proud, only to find out we got the wrong ones. We got "Horse Clams" and they are too tough to eat. Oh well!!! Try again.

The cruise ships are coming into port now and the town is overrun with tourists. Jerry smoked his fish today and I can hardly wait to sample it.

June 25th Bud had a very bad night and will be transferred to Anchorage tomorrow.

June 26th 10:45 and we are at the hospital awaiting the helicopter for the transfer and then we will drive up to Anchorage ourselves. Jerry and I talked with Bud's doctor yesterday and he stated "he doesn't have much lung reserve remaining and it's just a matter of time."

Jackie flew up with Bud and Jerry drove Buds pick-up and I the van (Bud insisted he have his truck in Anchorage so when he got out of the hospital he would have it to come back to Homer). It was a beautiful drive, but I must say Bud being so sick has taken the spirit out of doing any fun things.

June 29th and Jackie was told today that Bud has approximately 3 weeks to live. I will call her tomorrow and we will drive back to Anchorage on Sunday.

Back at work tonight and one of the nurses told of having a grizzly in her yard trying to get at her puppies and one shot in the air drove it off at least for now. Her place is about 6 miles from the village of Homer. News about Bud is the same, rested better last night but had a rough day. Jerry went salmon fishing today and no luck again.

We are putting an extension phone from Bud and Jackie's trailer to ours. We can keep in touch with Jackie and also take any of their calls. Weather here has finally warmed up but the spruce pollen is really bad and I really think it may be the culprit for all the respiratory problems.

July 1, and we drove down to the Spit after I got off work; it looks like a tent/trailer/motor home city. I think everyone from Anchorage is here for the 4th weekend and the weather is "beautiful"; what a change. We called and talked to Jackie this morning and Bud is somewhat better (not on respirator yet), but still very poor. We will wait and go to Anchorage on the 4th (late afternoon) and stay for a few days.

We went fishing with Tom and Jean Schroeder today. We met them five years ago when they came to Florida. Bud and Jackie had introduced us. We went out about 18 miles into the Cook Inlet, beautiful warm day. I finally caught a halibut, small one but a fish never the less. I also got a "cod fish". We were fishing in about 150 feet of water and pulling up a 6 pound fish seems like a hundred pounds. Jerry didn't catch any and now he knows how it feels, but he is going on the big boat tomorrow to fish for the big ones. I am going with Tom and we are flying over to McNeil River in hopes of viewing the bears. Tom flies as a Fish and Game Pilot to survey the salmon population and I am fortunate to be able to go along.

What a day!!! I met Tom at his office and then we drove down to the lake where the plane is (sea plane). It was a beautiful day and we started out flying west across the Cook Inlet; we needed to go 80 to 90 miles to reach McNeil River. It was absolutely beautiful up in the air, but we ran into a fog bank and when the pilot radioed McNeil he was told that it was zero visibility over there. We turned south and surveyed several bays and inlets looking for fish, very exciting ride. The plane turns on its side so Tom can see the water, especially around the shoreline looking for salmon. We flew between, around and over the mountains. I saw Exxon's area for rehabilitation for marine life that has been affected by the earlier oil spill; mostly sea otters were kept here. We flew over several villages that are across the bay, including Seldovia, China Poot, Cape Douglas and Halibut Cove. The villages are remote and only reached by boat or plane. After all the flying in every position but normal, I never got sick and really experienced a chance of a life time. When the weather improves I still hope to get the chance to go and film the bears.

Jerry caught a 25 pound halibut and a very large octopus which he gave away. He had a real good day too! He saw puffins, seals and he hooked into a real big fish that bent his pole way down and snapped the line. He is getting to look like a real "Alaskan." He still hasn't shaven.

RED  ~  THE OLD SALTY DOG

July 4$^{th}$ and we drove to Anchorage to see Bud. He really has lost ground the last week and doesn't look good at all.

July 5$^{th}$, and Bud had a bad night and now has pneumonia and is too weak to eat so has a feeding tube in now. We went up twice and stayed late with Jackie; finally convinced her to go out for something to eat. Jackie is really looking tired.

July 6$^{th}$. We took the van in for an alignment and then up to see Bud before heading back to Homer. I feel he is giving up. We made our reservations for departing for home. We leave here a month from now. We are taking the train from

Portage through the mountains to Whittier (van goes on the train) then we will board the Ferry for the 9 hour trip through Prince William Sound to reach Valdez.

July 7th. Bud was put on the respirator today. His outlook is poor. His entire family is with him and we are the only ones left in camp. We haven't been able to fish these past few days due to oil being found in Cook Inlet.

July 10th no word on Bud today, so no news is good news.

A day off and we're going to pack up some boxes to send back home and just goof off today! We'll go down to the Spit and take some pictures. Yesterday a motor home ended up in the harbor.

'HARBOR' ON THE SPIT

July 11th. Went to Anchorage today. No improvement in Bud. We really hate to see him like this, but then again feel fortunate to share his last days. It will take nothing short of a miracle for him to come out of this. I think Bud is at the point of either having to fight harder or let go. We treasure all of our good times of the past few years and I feel now that we were truly sent here on a mission to help Bud and Jackie during their difficult time. We left for Homer and got back to camp at 8 pm.

July 13th, had a great adventure today; went across the bay to Halibut Cove with Tom and Jean in their boat. It's so quaint there; if you can imagine neat cabins nestled in the mountains with a beautiful aqua cove in the center. We ate at the one and only place to eat, The Saltry. They only serve exotic food that you can't get anywhere else. We had salmon fixed everyway possible, zucchini stuffed with shrimp and rice, marinated halibut and more. The trip was great and visiting there was like no place we had ever seen to compare it with. The cabins are connected by wooden walkways that wind around the cliffs. Some of the residents are fulltime and others are aspiring painters or authors. It is one of those places that you dream about and would like to stay forever.

THE SALTRY

I worked last night and all was quiet. Doug and Lil called and they are in Fairbanks. We will meet them at the hospital in Anchorage on Monday. The pink salmon are now running in the fishing hole and still very little commercial fishing due to the oil spill.

LIL, JERRY AND I

Went to Anchorage yesterday and stopped to fish on the Kenai River on the way up. I got two sockeye on and lost both of them. They really put up a fight and I guess I need to keep the tip of my pole up.

Bud is about the same, but did require a tracheotomy. Doug and Lil followed us back to Homer, with a stop at the "Bird House". It's raining today and Doug and Lil are in Jackie's trailer and we all slept in. Took them on a sight seeing tour and then came back and had deep fried halibut.

I mailed 3 boxes back home today, mostly of things brought and not used. Cost $50.00, boy that hurt, but we had to make room for all our fish and items that we bought here. Rained again and we spent our day getting water for the trailer and tomorrow everyone else is going to dig clams across the bay while I go to work. I work this weekend and next and that's it. We leave here August 6th and I need the last week to pack.

July 21st, we had another extra special day. We went out in the big boat, left the harbor around 8:30 am and went to the head of the bay; some 20 to 30 miles. We pulled the skiff behind and anchored the boat and the 6 of us went ashore in the skiff to go clamming for "butter clams". We used rake forks and dug till we were all "dug out" and came back with four 5 gallon buckets full. On the way back we sighted a killer whale and headed back to begin the job of cleaning and eating clams.

KACHEMAK BAY

July 22nd, midnight and I just got home from work to a big plate of fried clams that Jerry prepared and so good!!! We heard from Jackie today and Bud took some chicken broth, first food in a long time and first good news too! Tomorrow Jerry will can the clams. It's getting darker earlier now and each day we lose minutes. The moose haven't been seen for several weeks, so they must have left for the hills.

July 24th, drove to Anchorage again, raining most of the day. We went to the hospital and Bud was very tired and we didn't stay long. They have been trying to wean him off the ventilator without much success. We told Bud today that we would be leaving for home Aug. 6th and he shrugged his eyebrows in a look of disappointment. He had not been off the ventilator and had a poor night. We said our goodbyes to Jackie and went and picked up Mandy (she had to go to the beauty parlor for a clip). I think we were the ones who got "clipped." $35.00 for a haircut, which is twice what we pay in Florida.

We stopped and camped on the Kenai River, caught 2 fish and looked forward to our next day of fishing.

July 26th; we fished all day, and not one was caught. We stopped and took an afternoon nap and went down for several more hours and still no luck. Went out for supper and fell exhausted into bed for 2nd night of camping. The next day I got one on and off it went. I've decided I had better stick to something I can do and it sure isn't catching salmon. Got back to camp and Tom had left a message that we would be going back to McNeil River in the next few days.

Bud has been able to be off the ventilator for a few hours at a time. I work the next three days and that's it. I'm going to miss all the people here. They have been so nice and helpful and I've learned new ways of doing old things and sure do appreciate the opportunity for the experience.

We will winterize the 5th wheel and spend these last 5 days in Homer trying to preserve all our memories. Tuesday I fly with Tom and the bush pilot to McNeil River (weather permitting).

August 1st and no flying; zero visibility, so did laundry instead and Tom said we would try again in a couple of days. Today we moved out of the 5th wheel and will spend two nights in Bud and Jackie's trailer. The 5th wheel is winterized and the project took all day. I didn't believe we could fit everything back into the van, but we did!

It is a beautiful sunny day and our last full day here. Tom just called and we leave shortly for McNeil River.

4:30 pm, what a day. We flew across the inlet and right over Mt. Augustine, so close that one could smell the sulphur and it gave me an idea of what the moon surface might be like. The volcano was all lava, ashes and no growth. We then flew on across to Cape Douglas which is also a volcano, but much higher and had snow and glaciers on its surface. We spotted a large bull moose standing in a meadow with a huge rack. We did some fish surveying (plane on its side) and headed for McNeil River. Winds out of the west were very strong and a couple of times we hit air pockets and would drop what seemed like a few hundred feet (not to good on the stomach). I didn't get sick, but close to it. We started seeing bears and I do mean

BIG bears all over the place. I do believe this was the most exciting adventure that I have ever done. Try and imagine the beauty of the river and falls and bears everywhere. I didn't know where to start filming. I spotted this large one just sitting on a big rock in the middle of the stream and he looked like he was just waiting for a salmon to jump into his arms. Other bears were actively involved in jumping in and coming out with big fish in their mouths. This is the McNeil River Falls that has been on the National Geographic and Discovery Channels.

The beauty of this area is breathtaking and even more so when viewed from the air and I will always be grateful to Tom for giving me this once-in-a-lifetime experience.

Jerry picked me up at the plane dock and we continued to make ready for closing everything up. We packed the last few things before heading up to Anchorage to see Bud before heading to Portage and the train. It was extremely hard to leave Homer again, but we will treasure our memories and look forward to another trip here in the future.

We spent the night in Anchorage and had a long discussion with Jackie regarding Bud's progress (or lack of). He now has another infection and if he hangs on like he has, the doctor has talked about Jackie considering nursing home placement. That would kill him for sure. Bud at this point remains in ICU and on the respirator.

August 6th, Went back to the hospital, very hard to choke back tears in front of Bud, but we managed well until we said goodbye to Jackie at the elevator. We know in our hearts we will never see him again. (Not in this life anyway).

12:30 and we are now in line waiting to drive our vehicle onto the train at Portage for the trip through the mountain tunnels to the coast of Whittier in Prince William Sound. It is a very warm and sunny day.

3 pm and leaving Whittier on the ferry. The train ride was exciting through long tunnels in the mountains, so dark in that there was no hint of what lightness would be like. The town of Whittier is a World War II military base and there remain several very large buildings that once provided housing for the service men.

Whittier has a small harbor nestled in the mountains and our ferry *The Bartlett*, was already in port. We boarded the ship by driving our van onto the lower deck and we went topside. Mandy had to stay in the vehicle and I'm sure she didn't like that. The first part of the trip was beautiful and warm. We saw a very large colony of kittiwakes, pilot whales and seals. We also saw many islands with oil stained beaches. After an hour or so the nice weather turned to a cold rain and we started coming into icebergs several miles before we came to the Columbia Glacier.

The visibility was very poor, almost like an ice fog and we managed to see just the base of the majestic glacier. We were in a field of "icebergs". The icebergs were covered with oil at the bases, and we noted several bergs with seals sitting on top of them. The rest of the trip was mostly socked in with rain and fog and very cold (29 degrees). We arrived in Valdez at 10 pm (didn't take as long due to not spending time at the glacier). We found a spot to park the van and went to sleep.

Woke up to rain again and it's hard to see the town which lies surrounded by mammoth mountains. We drove around to the Alaska Pipe Line Terminal. This is where the 800 mile pipeline ends and the oil is then shipped from here. It was just a short distance from here that the tanker Exxon Valdez ran aground on Bligh Reef in northeastern Prince William Sound resulting in the largest oil spill in United States waters. The oil terminal was impressive and something to see.

Due to the awful weather there wasn't much to see or do in Valdez, so we started our journey north towards Tok, Alaska. We stopped to scout out some fishing spots along the way and came upon huge bear tracks and along side were little bear tracks, not a good place for us to be!! We left while we had the chance. Stopped for the night along the Little Tok River and are soothed to sleep by the sound of water splashing over the rocks.

July 9th. Drove from Tok to Whitehorse yesterday, beautiful weather and roads not to bad. Saw a large eagle. We are at the same campground that we stopped at on the way up. It's 9 am and Jerry is taking a shower and I'm next. I'm sitting at the picnic table and just enjoying my coffee, writing; it's sunny but cool, (50 degrees). We start out for Watson Lake today.

We had quite an experience last night, or rather early this am. We stopped at a beautiful creek last night around 7:30 pm and we were about 10 miles west of Watson Lake, Yukon. We had backed the van up to the creek edge so we could hear the water run during the night. We played a game of gin and turned in for the night. We awoke to Mandy's bark and the sound of a car and sat up to see what it was. We first saw a figure of one man standing by the creek and then we had the fright of our lives as 5 or 6 figures of men approached the front of our van, one shone a light on our license plates and they stood there talking loudly for what seemed like forever. Part of the group walked back to the car where a radio was playing very loud and they stood there appearing to decide what to do next. One person walked around the van and then, thank God they got in the car and drove off. It was 3 am and we felt we had lucked out and got up and drove to Watson Lake and parked for the rest of the night in a well lighted area.

We left Watson Lake and began driving the worst roads yet…about 150 miles of dirt and mud. We arrived at Laird Hot Springs, got a camp site and took our walk to the springs and relaxed in the soothing water. On the walk back we filmed a young moose and we had seen a young black bear earlier.

Tomorrow we will head towards Edmonton, Canada and so we leave this wonderful country with thoughts already of when we will be able to return "One More Time".

# BUD

May 8th, 1990 and we leave again for another trip to Alaska. This is our 3rd trip. Every trip is different and filled with adventure. We will spend the entire summer and hope our fishing expertise improves. We look forward to seeing familiar faces and to once again see our friend Bud, who is back in Homer and doing better than most of us ever thought possible.

Our day yesterday was putting a lot of miles on and we stopped at a rest area just south of Birmingham, Alabama (we are still living in Florida). The events of the day included: Mandy stepping in bubble gum during one of her pit stops, (that was fun to clean) next she decided to have a small seizure (hadn't had one since last July) and then I cracked my knee cap by hitting it on the closet (hurts a lot) but I don't have time for such things so it will just have to go away. We are now having coffee at the picnic table. The sun is out and it's probably 75 degrees.

Day 3 went 680 miles yesterday (we can't wait to get there). This morning it is cool and raining and we are about 70 miles east of Kansas City, Kansas on Interstate 70 and I still have shorts on.

11:30, remember what I said about having shorts on? Well forget it! We are about 80 miles south of Council Bluffs, Iowa on Interstate 29 and it is approximately 50 degrees, cloudy and windy and my shorts have retired for jogging pants. 6:30 pm and temperature has fallen to 47 degrees and expected to go to 32 degrees. We are at Sioux Falls, South Dakota and headed for the Canadian border. We are going to have our homemade clam chowder and that should warm us up. The area that we've been in is miles and miles of farm land with most of the fields plowed and planted.

We spent the night at a rest area 50 miles south of Fargo, North Dakota. It was 27 degrees when we woke up. Making coffee with our little stove soon took off the chill. (We are in our van; same as last year). It was so cold that Mandy was trying to bury her food under the rug, guess she thought she had to get her winter supply put away. Now it is 8:30 and we are headed north, sun is out and in spite of the cold it really is beautiful. All you see for miles is a patch work of crops being planted and these people must be ministers of God to survive out here and be at the mercy of the elements to raise food for all the rest of us.

We spent the night parked by a gas station about 50 miles south of Saskatoon, Saskatchewan. It is cold outside but we were warm under the quilts. The trees here are just starting to bud. Yesterday we saw a lot of Canadian geese and also 8 to 10 mule deer that ran out in front of us. 1 pm, and we've had our lunch and heading up Highway 16 in Alberta, Canada towards Edmonton. Guess we're going to have to break down and get a motel tonight (need a shower). The campgrounds aren't open this early. We are starting to see more tree growth and hills as we leave the vast farm land behind. Price of gas is 55.4 per liter; costly right? Exchange on our dollar was 18 cents per dollar. We stopped at a shopping mall and cigarettes were $3.99 per pack or $33.49 per carton; good thing we don't smoke. Now you know why we bring most of our supplies with us.

We really went through inspection at Canadian Customs, they got right in the van and opened every case and cabinet; under the bed, in the dirty clothes bag, coolers and I finally asked them what they were looking for and was told "hand guns". They gave up after a while and we continued down the road.

May 12th our journey continues. We spent the night in a motel in White Court (NW of Edmonton). The bath felt wonderful and we enjoyed the change. It's now 9 am and we have heard that there is considerable snowfall ahead. Grand Prairie got 6 to 8 inches last night and that's where we're headed. We have left the sun behind and it's very cold and windy.

We are in our kind of country, hills, lakes, rivers and spruce trees and the only signs of man is the utility lines and road signs. It is so beautiful and untamed. The van has the smell of fresh brewed coffee and is enjoyed by both of us as we continue our journey.

12:10 pm and now we are in snow, just northwest of Grand Prairie and this is much sooner then we usually hit snow other than the Rocky Mountains. Snow is getting deeper and everything looks beautiful from inside a warm van. Lunch consisted of hot tomato soup and grilled cheese sandwiches. I'm getting to be an expert in holding things on the stove while bumping down the road. We just caught a glimpse of the majestic Rocky Mountains (all covered with snow). We saw one deer and one coyote.

COYOTE

Mile marker 245 and we are on gravel roads now and real dusty in spite of the snow. Roads are really rough and in places have slid down the mountainside. We spotted our first moose and right on the road, now we really feel like we're back home in Alaska and we're still in British Columbia.

May 13<sup>th</sup> and we just come through Ft. Nelson and the road lived up to its reputation; switchbacks, narrow mountain climbing and snow! We camped at mile marker 346 (from Dawson Creek) at Tetsa River Provincial Park. Park wasn't officially open but there were a couple of vehicles there already so we stayed too!

We saw caribou and a porcupine at the camp and woke up to find our water cooler and ice chest froze that we had left outside. We were warm as usual. Mandy is being her usual "good dog" and seems to remember being here before; it doesn't take her long to get under the comforter at night. This morning it is cold, but sunny as we awake in nature's bedroom of beauty, with snow, but you sure feel refreshed when you wash your face and brush your teeth outside. We are surrounded by the Canadian Rockies.

We stopped at Summit Lodge, the highest point on the Alaska Highway, had coffee and toast (first time we have been in a restaurant on this trip) it's starting to really snow now, really large flakes. We stopped and chopped ice from a lake for our coolers. Passed by some mountain sheep and filmed them from about 8 feet away.

We covered 131 miles today, winding in and around the mountains, snow and all. We stopped at Laird Hot Springs Provincial Park, found our camp site, had lunch and headed for a soak in the hot springs.

We sure do enjoy our stops at the hot springs, it has become a favorite. The hot mineral waters sooth away the aches from the long trip. We came back from the spring, made a fire, played gin, visited with people from Jacksonville, Florida and then cooked our supper (polish sausage and beans) over our open fire. It started to rain and we retreated to the security of the van once again and ready to retire at 9 pm. The hot springs really takes a lot out of you and makes one sleep like a baby. We haven't seen any bears so far.

May 14, and we slept good (not as cold), had our coffee and started down the road. Met Mrs. Moose out for her morning stroll and she was a little close for comfort to our front bumper as were doing 45 to 50 miles per hour. We are traveling on very poor roads and through an area of burn that I mentioned in previous chapters. You see nothing but burn area for approximately 50 miles.

Just came through Watson Lake, Yukon Territory, roads are a little better, colder again and lakes still froze over. Our destination today is Whitehorse and weather permitting we will make it! 12:05 pm forget what I said about the roads being better, we just came through mud!

We are now at a campground in Whitehorse. Was able to do the laundry, but showers won't be open for a couple of days yet. So! Guess it's another day before we shower again. At the rate were going we should be in Anchorage on the 16th, which means it took us 9 days, but we still have another day to get to Homer.

We have met a lot of interesting people along the road and somehow we all end up at the same campground to compare notes of "how bad the road was" or what kind of vehicle troubles one may have encountered.

Good morning!!"BURR', it's cold here. We left Whitehorse and went on to Haines Junction and ate breakfast out, tasted real good, we each had 2 eggs, bacon, toast and coffee…cost $13.00. Ouch! When we woke up in Whitehorse; we were covered with snow. The roads were snowy till we got just about to Haines Junction. 11 am and heading on toward Kluane Lake, which lies deep in the mountains with ice fields all around. The lake sits in Kluane National Park which is all natural and undeveloped. The lake is approximately 154 miles square. It is a very cold day and rains off and on (which is usually the case) around this area. We have about 20 miles or so before we catch our first glimpse of the lake. The road is bad, it's like a roller coaster filled with pot holes. The mountains look out of character with their peaks cut off by the low cloud cover. Our destination today is Tok, Alaska; another 300 miles or so.

KLUANE LAKE

We have been on the roughest roads of the entire trip for the last 90 miles and can only go about 40 miles an hour. We just stopped and took a nature break (out in nature) and when we were driving off a wolf crossed in front of us, he had to have heard us talking when we were stopped and I was disappointed at not having the camera ready and knowing that wolves are not solitary creatures, made me wonder as to how many others there may have been in the vicinity.

Crossed into Alaska, weather has warmed up a lot; 60 to 65 degrees and sunny, very unusual at least for us to encounter warm weather. Roads have improved and now we're about 50 miles from Tok. We just came across a bridge where the guard rails had come right out of the ground and the ground opened up leaving half the roadside gone. This valley is so warm that we're ready to shed the warm shirts and sweaters, but will wait to see what the next few miles bring.

4 pm and we're in Tok, still warm, called Carla and it was as warm here as it was in Grand Rapids, Michigan. We decided to give our tired old bones a break and checked into a motel; real nice and new and only $35.00. Rates will be going up shortly. The view from our window is, picture postcard perfect, and wish I could paint so I could relish the memory forever. After you have been on the road for 4 or 5 days, you really appreciate what a real bath feels like.

May 16th, slept good and woke up at 5 am. Started for Anchorage, cold out, but sunny, went for our breakfast at a little road house about 60 miles from Tok. We were hoping to see the "official mascot" (a horse) that comes out to your car to greet you but the owner said he sent someone to pick up the horse from his winter quarters and they brought back the wrong horse. Last year the horse came out to the van while we were inside and he peeked in the windows and we thought Mandy was going to crash through the window. She had never seen a horse and especially one with his nose against the window.

We are still heading for Anchorage and winding our way through the mountains with glaciers in the distance. We have seen 2 herds of caribou, 2 moose and 1 elk.

May 17th, arrived in Anchorage yesterday around 4 pm. We talked with Bud and Jackie in Homer. Bud sounded short of breath so we didn't talk to long. We will get supplies for our summer in Homer and then head down the highway tomorrow.

Need to pick a few more items this morning and begin the 5 to 6 hour drive to Homer. We stopped at Cooper Landing for lunch and to visit with people we had met on previous trips. We finally arrived in Homer at 5:30 pm and after nine months reunite with our dear friends, Bud and Jackie. I will say Bud looked better than I was expecting, but feel in my heart his days are a precious few. He seems to have given up and his only effort is to get from his chair to the table and to bed. So hopefully this summer we can get some goals for him to achieve and take one day at a time.

Today is a work day, got to open up the 5th wheel, hook up water, turn on electric, gas and phone. Then unpack from the van to the 5th wheel. Each year I wonder how we manage to put all that we do in the van. 8:30 pm and finally done!! And now can think of more fun things, like fishing. Jackie and I went and got two racks of BBQ ribs and baked beans for supper (to tired to cook).

May 20th, slept good in our 5th wheel and we are very cozy. The only thing about a trailer this size (30 feet) is everything must be in its place or it can be a disaster. We need to go and get our fishing license because we plan on going fishing today! We will go on Bud's nephew's boat; the *Nakona* which is 44 feet long and is a commercial fishing boat. We feel fortunate to have the opportunity to go on the boat for halibut fishing.

What a day! Seas are really rough, even the stabilizers didn't help. It turned real cold and 3 out of the 4 of us got a little sea sick, but in spite of all that over 200 pounds of halibut was caught. One was 110 pounds and Jerry caught one at 50 pounds. I hooked on to the biggest fish ever; the drag wasn't set right and snap went the line. We came back to camp around 5:30 and then had to clean all the catch and now it was really freezing cold. Jackie fried up some fish while we cleaned the rest. "Yum, yum" and then we crashed. What a day. Tomorrow we will freeze and can it all.

Today is laundry and banking. I stopped by the hospital and so good to see old friends. I start May 25th, 3 to 1:30 am, 4 days a week. The present Head Nurse is gone on a 10 day vacation and she will be acting Director of Nurses when she returns and I'll try to do a good job in keeping the ER running smooth for the summer. Bud did not have a good day. His friends from Florida called and he could hardly talk to them.

We canned 48 jars of halibut yesterday. It was real cold in the gear shed when we started, but warmed up during the day.

ROSE IN THE GEAR SHED

It's going to get down to the low 30's tonight and cold and raining tomorrow. Jerry and I will take tomorrow to visit the area and see familiar sites and on Thursday will go 70 miles north to go hooligan fishing.

Went back up to the hospital today to sign my 3 months contract and work this Friday, Saturday , Sunday and Monday. This is the busiest week-end of the year. We went down to the Spit and stopped at the ferry office to inquire about our trip to Kodiak this August. We want to see the outdoor theater drama of "Cry of the Wild Ram", which is presented every August. We came back to camp and made out long over due post cards.

Well! Vacation is over and at 3 pm it's back to work for me. We caught our catch of hooligans yesterday and toured the area of the village of Kenai. This area had a lot of volcano ash from Mr. Redoubt, which is just across the Cook Inlet.

Today was sunny and warm and we returned to Homer by 8 pm. Our exhausted bodies fell into bed at 9.

I survived my first day back at work, things hadn't changed much and a lot of the same people were there from last year. We went down to the Spit this morning and it is wall to wall people, here for the Memorial weekend. Tides are really low and it's excellent clam digging. The waters are calm for fishing. We also saw our first moose in camp this morning.

Last night at work made up for the slow one a couple of shifts ago, 20 patients, with just me and a paramedic. The next morning Jerry and I went out for breakfast and some picture taking of all the activity on the Spit.

May 28th a busy night at work again. 18 patients and just me! But we made it. Had a doctor in from Salt Lake City as our "rent a Doc" for the week-end, a great guy to work with; fast and patients loved him too! A lot of doctors rotate through here (all ER docs) they come up for a combined vacation-fishing and work. In addition to being the nurse, you are the ward clerk, telephone operator, pharmacist, respiratory therapist, EKG tech, phlebotomist and transporter to x-ray and to bed when admitted. GEE!! It makes me wonder why I left Florida- "just kidding". Although it's an eye opener and makes you appreciate both jobs. It really is a different world here.

What a day! Ate lunch out, went fishing (no luck) so we went down to "Lands End", a bar and restaurant and ordered a bucket of steamer clams....so good. Then we went to Jose's, a Mexican restaurant, split a burrito and two margaritas. I guess we felt like treating ourselves royally.

Slept in today and then went for a ride high up on the mountain so we could view the Spit, bay and mountains from the most beautiful view ever. It is called Diamond Ridge. We saw our first baby moose; it couldn't have been more than a few days old and stuck very close to mamma. We are always so excited as if we've never seen one before. Came back to camp and checked in with Bud and Jackie. Bud was not having a good day and in checking his lungs, he wasn't moving much air and seemed more anxious. Also he has been on a new medicine, Prozac, for the past nine days which was supposed to elevate his mood. It seems to have increased his anxiety which increases his demand for oxygen. He agreed to go up to the hospital for a check and the doctor increased his Prednisone and took him off the Prozac. His chest x-ray was not as good as the last, but we were able to bring him home and that of course made him happy. We brought Bud home and then went down to the fishing hole again (no luck again), but had to chuckle when a kid about 10 or 12 years old came up to Jerry and said "Hey, Gramps, have you gotten any bites?" Makes you know that we're definitely not getting any younger.

Saw a momma moose and her twins today, right in town in someone's yard, chewing on the tree. The moose here are respected and left alone and are expected to go wherever they please. They hold up traffic and you just stop and wait for them to move on. It's really strange. Bud's doctor called me today and said the radiologist read the x-ray as an infiltrate in the right upper lobe, so now we have him on antibiotics and he will have a repeat x-ray in one week. He did get out yesterday for a short ride and an ice cream cone, so that was encouraging.

We are really surprised as to how much this area has grown in the past year and on the weekend the town's population seems to increase by thousands. After having traveled most of Alaska, I certainly understand why this is the most beautiful part of Alaska.

It's June already! It was a busy night at work again. Bud is feeling a bit better. Saw two eagles today and another moose and her baby. It's been really nice dry weather, 61 degrees for a high and 45 degrees for a low. Mosquitoes are out and 4 times bigger than the Florida species, but because of the cold are more dormant and less aggressive. I broke down and used the vacuum cleaner today. Hey! This is supposed to be my vacation too!

We awoke yesterday to Mandy's low bark and looked out to see a big moose right next to the window. Bud is feeling much better and got out for lunch on the Spit today. It is so good to see him up and about. Tomorrow we are going north for about 40 miles to fish for king salmon in Deep Creek, hope to get some sun too!(miss the sun, but not the heat) make sense? Sometimes I wonder why we're not content to just stay home, but then again appreciate the opportunity to be here too! I feel very strong about doing what were doing now, while we have our health and are able to enjoy, and always wish my family and friends could also see this beautiful country.

We had quite a day yesterday, went exploring about 50 miles north of here, and fished for King Salmon on Deep Creek and very frustrating to be able to see the big fish but they wouldn't bite. But we had fun anyway. It was a beautiful day. We took some great still pictures and some video too. Saw 6 moose and even got a little sunburn.

June 5$^{th}$, went down to the Spit and no one catching fish so we went out to east end road and stopped at a couple of bars and met a lot of interesting people. Decided we needed to get to bed early for a change. We were jolted out of our beds at 3:22 am with earthquake tremors measuring 4.1 on the Richter Scale. When you're sitting on a bluff high above the water and in a trailer, that 4.1 feels like a 10 and hope we never feel that experience again. Mr. Moose was outside our 5$^{th}$ wheel again this morning, I went outside to throw out some bread to the squirrels and heard a "snap" only to look up and see this big creature a few feet away. The moose here are about as plentiful as squirrels.

Jerry has a bad cold so he is staying away from Bud. We took Bud back to the hospital for his scheduled x-ray and he is doing fine. I now have the next four days off and if Jerry gets to feeling better we will go camping about 50 miles north of here for a fishing weekend.

June 13$^{th}$ spent the last 4 days camping. We drove up to Anchor Point to the Anchor River the first night and fished again for king salmon with no luck, then drove up to Deep Creek and spent the night along the creek. Fished the next day for 5 hours straight and the only thing we caught were 3 Irish Lords and you don't eat them. Still no King! We saw lots of eagles and the weather was really cold and windy. We spent Monday night along the "Kasilof River", saw a moose swim across the river. Tuesday morning drove on up to Crooked Creek and everyone else from the 48 states was there too! Very few fish were being caught. One got on my line and just as quick got off. We came back to the van and ate supper at 11pm and then went back down to the creek till 2 am and still no fish. We have chased the elusive King throughout every stream in south central Alaska! We woke up to rain and came back home to do laundry.

To update you all on prices here! Went to grocery store yesterday; loaf of bread $2.49, then we stopped at a bakery to get our sour dough garlic bread...$3.08, so two loaves of bread $5.57, cheap huh? It won't be long and we'll have to make a supply run to Anchorage. This morning it is beautiful and we sit here with our coffee looking out across the bay to the glaciers.

GREWINGK GLACIER AND KACHEMAK BAY

Jerry started to smoke the salmon last night, so won't be long and we'll taste delicious smoked salmon. (Note! The salmon was given to us, not caught by us). Don't give up hope on our fishing abilities as they will improve in later chapters.

While driving home at 2:20 in the morning on June 16th I encountered Mrs. Moose out for a late stroll with her 2 babies. I'm on my 3 days off and yesterday we tried King fishing once again and once again "no luck". Had a new experience last night, we went to the movies and saw *Bird on a Wire*. It was excellent, but the theater was not your usual one! It was built like a barn with seats only half way down to the screen. We could set in front and still be in the middle of the room. The walls were bare concrete (no fancy velour wall coverings) and it was freezing inside.

Finally! A sunny day and warm. We haven't done anything exciting this past week. Well I haven't, but Jerry has; he seems to be prone to bad luck. We were coming out of Jose's Restaurant and a kid on a bike ran into him, knocking him down, and guess what? He broke his hand, yup the right one, he has only had 4 different surgeries on that same arm and now a broken hand too! And oh yes the kid was the owner's son and they agreed to pay all bills. So Jerry is in a short arm splint for the next 4 to 6 weeks.

Yesterday was another experience and one I don't want to do again. Jerry picked me up from work at 1:30 am and we drove approximately 50 miles north to Ninilchik. There is a state recreational area on the beach. Actually you just park where you can and all that's provided is an outside privy. There must have been 500 plus vehicles of every description, all there for razor clamming. We went to sleep for 5 hours and got up, had coffee and followed the mass of people out to sea literally. The tide was going out fast and would end up a minus 4.5 tide, exposing a sand bar about ½ mile out. When I say sand bar, it really is "glacier mud". To get a razor clam is a challenge and I usually love challenges, but not when I have to get muddy and wet from head to toe. A razor clam is oval in shape and gets really big and our largest was approximately 10 inches long. The procedure is (1) see a hole (2) put a small shovel down deep next to the hole and (3) quickly put your hand in the hole and hopefully grab on to the clams neck and pull and dig with the other hand. I would shovel and Jerry would take his left hand and dig. We ended up with 24 clams and sore bodies, wet and muddy. Now we clean them and eat for supper.

RAZOR CLAM

June 25th we cleaned our clams after getting lessons from Jackie and then Jackie fried them in cracker crumbs and bacon grease. We really pigged out and then froze the rest for chowder. We went down to the harbor around 9 pm to see the fishing fleet come in. Today was the opening day of commercial sockeye salmon and viewing the fishing fleet coming back into the harbor is quite a sight to see. They can only fish on Mondays and Fridays from 6 am to 6 pm. Tomorrow we're going steamer clamming. They are much easier than razor clams and also I think they are better eating too.

Boy, are we tired, we left the harbor early and it took over an hour to reach the clam beach at the head of Kachemak Bay. There were so many clams we thought we were in a candy store. We will be eating clams all summer. We also got mussels and came back home and everyone pigged out once again. The next day I made linguini with clams and we froze about 20 bags of steamers and mussels and will cut up the rest to can.

We cleaned up 10 gallons of clams this morning and tomorrow we will can. If you think I'm up here just relaxing; think again! This is work!!! Jerry's hand remains swollen and in the splint and he has a huge black and blue area on this thigh where he was knocked to the ground. Bud has been feeling really good lately and increasing his activity a little, his appetite has improved too. We plan on making a trip to Anchorage the 9th of July for supplies and R & R.

Another member of our family is supporting the local economy. Mandy had to go in and get a "D&C". This 12 year old, post-menopausal pup started to bleed early this am. Took her to the vet and she had surgery to remove a polyp about the size of my thumb, but everything is ok and she is back to her normal self. Here's hoping no one else gets sick. Bud continues to improve and is getting out more often.

Weather here has been warm and sunny. We've had two tragic plane crashes during this past week, one with a mother and daughter from Orlando, Florida that crashed into a mountain and another that went into the water across the bay with 2 people aboard. The one that hit the mountain killed 5 people.

July 6th, we had a good July 4th, worked last night and very busy. Mandy is doing fine. I work the next 3 days and then it's off to Anchorage to get "citified." We will go sockeye salmon fishing on the Kenai River on the way back. We have been gone from Florida for 2 months now and in some ways it seems a lot longer. We will leave here on August 24th to start home and meet our son and his family in Edmonton.

July 11, just got back after spending 3 days in Anchorage. Had a great trip, went to dinner, did our shopping and did a lot of sight seeing on the way there and back. Anchorage is like any other large city you may find in the lower 48. We stopped and went salmon fishing on the Kenai River, but the run was extremely slow. Fishing is way down this year compared to previous years.

I spent all morning on the phone, checking on airline procedures for supplying oxygen to passengers in flight. I found that there is a way for Bud to have his oxygen while changing planes too, should he decide to come to Florida this winter. He is totally dependent on oxygen now.

Had a wonderful day fishing with Tom and Jean. I caught a 35 and a 20 pound halibut and was that ever fun!! Then we went to Halibut Cove (across the bay from Homer). We ate a delicious dinner of exotic food, the only thing familiar was a loaf of bread and even that was very different. The bread was made with sunflower seeds. As I have mentioned before, Halibut Cove is a quaint paradise that lies behind the mountains that face the bay. Artists from all over the world stay there in the summer months, tucked back in the mountains in quaint little studios. It is the only place that I've ever seen paintings done with octopus ink.

HALIBUT COVE

July 18th. Picture if you can our camp at Morgan's Landing, a State Park high above the Kenai River, near Sterling, Alaska and that's where we are at present. We're sitting at our camp site, having coffee, reading the paper and it is about 75 degrees. We are inland and away from the glaciers, so it's much warmer here. We came here yesterday and the elusive sockeye are finally running up the river to spawn and we hope to catch a few. There are a lot of other people here trying their luck too! It was so nice to sit around our camp fire last night and then the couple camped next to us brought over some of their freshly caught salmon and grilled it over the fire; delicious!! We are convinced that bumming around the country is the life for us. We'll fish here today and go back to Homer tomorrow as I am scheduled to work a 5 day stretch.

We fished till late yesterday and I finally landed my sockeye, in fact I got 2, only one was not legal because the lure was in the face and not in the mouth. They sure are a fighting fish and my arms and shoulders feel it today. Jerry wasn't as lucky, very difficult for him to fish with his left hand. The weather is cooler in Homer due to the glaciers runoff.

Just finished 4 out of my 5 shifts and we are looking forward to Tuesday when we can go up to the river again. Took Bud up to the hospital again, he wasn't moving much air and they did lab work and chest x-ray again. He stayed long enough to get some medicine and was able to go home again. It is a day to day with him and it sure is painful to watch him suffer.

July 27th and back at work and all I can think about is fishing. I'm really hooked on fishing for sockeye. We came back last night from the Kenai River and I caught 3. We are going back this Sunday. Bud is feeling a little better and actually asked questions as to how his oxygen needs could be met if he went back to Florida. I really hope he comes to Florida; it will be a long cold winter here for him. Our time here is going fast, I have 19 more working days and we leave here Aug. 25th.

We are back camping at Morgan's Landing. It's 10:45 pm and I got 2 sockeye today, Jerry zero again. We arrived last night and will stay till Wednesday, we really enjoy this campground, and it is so relaxed and laid back. Everyone just finds a place to park, there is no designated sites. Part of the park is an old airstrip not being used as such and campers just line up and fill every available space. We have got this camping down to a science in our van. After this period of fishing we have to start canning all of our previous caught fish.

THE AUTHOR AND HER SALMON

It started raining about one week ago and seems to stay with us day after day; this is usual for August and will continue to rain till it turns to snow.

August 1ˢᵗ and we said goodbye to the Kenai River, had a great time, I caught 4 more fish which makes a total of 8 and Jerry finally caught 2, really difficult to do for him with one good hand and the other in a splint. We are on our way back to Homer; really need to clean up, its fun camping, but it's pretty bad when the dog smells better than we do! Now we get to can all our fish. It's still raining on and off and cool. The Alaska flower, Fireweed, is really out and the mountain sides are ablaze with the purple/red flowers.

There is so much to be said about the peace and solitude that one feels in this place, I guess part of it is, ones getting back in touch with the natural world and away from all the pressures that we usually bring on ourselves. The days are getting darker earlier, and it seems to be getting cooler. It's freezing at 6000 feet and soon "snow", so like the wild geese, it's getting time to migrate south for the winter. We really are ready to come home, but also feel a tug in our hearts in leaving here. This land seems to provide us the inner peace that is lacking in the fast paced life style of most of the lower 48.

Jerry has finished building the pump house for Bud, in spite of his injured hand, which is doing better now.

THE PUMP HOUSE

It is still raining and getting colder by the day. We are going to the Kenai River one more time next week. The big silver salmon are running. We canned our fish and got 48 jars. Our time is drawing near (14 more days) and of that I have only 4 days off.

August 14th and we just got back from spending 2 days on the River. It was beautiful weather and caught fish again. The dog and I got hair cuts and Jerry got a van check up for the long trip home. Yesterday the area had a 5.6 earthquake which we never felt as we were traveling down a gravel road. Last week the whole hospital shook with a tremor and wondering if Mt. Redoubt is going to blow its top again!

Our plans are to leave here the 24th and our destination will take us to Dawson City to see what it was like during the "Gold Rush Days".

This day started at 4 am, when we were awakened by Jackie, to come quick as something was wrong with Bud. On my arrival, Bud was in near respiratory arrest seated on the toilet. His color was ashen blue. I sent Jackie to dial 911 and lowered

Bud to the bathroom floor and there he lay with his head in my lap till the ambulance arrived. He made me promise not to allow any life support systems and when the ambulance crew arrived they respected his and Jackie's wishes. On arriving to the hospital his blood gases were incompatible with life, but he remained totally lucid and was admitted to a room to die with dignity, and the rest of the day will forever remain with all of us who were so close to him.

He was so peaceful and stated he was ready to go now and seemed to gain an inner strength which allowed him to get affairs in order and he spent the whole day going over his life with great stories and a very unique state of humor. He had us all laughing and if he goes out like this he has given us all a very special parting remembrance of him. I watched him sleep for 3 hours, very peaceful with little effort in his breathing. When he awoke he said "I'm ready to go, why is it taking so long? He further stated "I guess I have to get in line". Bud has only allowed IV's and oxygen and has refused anything else and we respect his wishes completely.

He seemed not to tire at all and I was in and out of his room all night and he was still telling me stories of his life experiences. We have learned to take each day as a gift with Bud and try not to wonder what tomorrow will bring. When I left at 11:30 pm he was very comfortable and relaxed.

August 18th, these last couple of days has been up and down with Bud and the last 8 hours he seems to be going down hill. During work tonight I was in and out of his room and could see him fail hour by hour.

Bud has left us and we shall always treasure these last days with him. We were called back to the hospital at 5:30 am and stayed till 8:30 am. He was still conscious, but slipped into a coma at 10 am. I returned to work at 2:50 pm, stopped to see Bud first and he died at 2:59. He just went to sleep as we held him in our arms. We get so few chances at knowing someone like Bud, and no one will ever come close to meaning what he has meant to us. Bud had lived most of his adult life in Alaska and he treasured his experiences of living in this wondrous land. He shared stories of his hunting, fishing, flying his own plane and his travels throughout Alaska when he worked building roads. When we left his hospital room, we never saw him again and that's the way he wanted it.

August 20th. Jackie is doing as well as one can during this sad time for her and will do fine once she gets all the business affairs done and can come to Florida for the winter. It has been very hard on her for the past year or so. We are all keeping busy with all the work to get camp closed and get Jackie back to Anchorage and us on our way home. Bud's wishes to be cremated were carried out yesterday and come spring his ashes will be taken by boat to be spread out on the mountain slopes and streams in Kachemak Bay. There was no service per Bud's request and he sure has us convinced that this is the way to do it.

August 25th, we camped at Scout Lake last night. I worked till 1:30 am. It's hard to say goodbye to all these great people. I will miss them very much. We're about 85 miles south of Anchorage, the mountains look so green until you get to the top and then they're bare rock with snow. The trees are turning yellow and the fireweed has lost almost all of its crimson flowers. It's cold and raining.

12:20 just came by white whales feeding on salmon around Turnagain Arm and stopped to film them. They were pure white Beluga whales. We stopped by to see the hybrid wolves on display in Palmer. They are beautiful animals and I got to film them. We also saw a huge bull moose just off the side of the road.

August 27th in the last 24 hours our journey took us into an area the likes of which we've never seen before. We left the Alaska Highway just east of Tok and took the Taylor Highway to Dawson City in the Yukon. It is a 6 hour trip to go approximately 150 miles. Now the term "highway" is a total false hood, the highway is all gravel and clay and the first 4 hours were unbelievably beautiful with high mountain driving, switch backs. Most of the time we were above the tree line (so high with no growth). It was cool and rainy and the gravel was turning to mud. As we neared the Canadian border, we really were at the "Top of the World" and that's what that point of this highway was called. Our transmission was beginning to smell, but it was so cold on the top, it cooled quickly. From the border to the Yukon River, was hair raising to put it mildly! We continued a few more miles enjoying the tundra and its remaining flowers, most of which are gone for this year in preparation for a long winter.

We are at a point 165 miles south of the Artic Circle and even with all this beauty it has a story of being an unforgiving environment. We continued on around shear cliffs with picturesque beauty below. (No guard rails). The enjoyment was soon to come to an end as we ran into thick fog. Remember, we're still on switch backs and the road now is a sea of muddy clay and now we can't see!! It was an experience that we're glad not to repeat, and once again the Lord watched over us.

We saw many sites of old gold mining days, capturing a lot on video. There were even some skeletons of large rigs used for dredging and their rusted remains lie exposed to the harsh elements of nature. We boarded the ferry for the ride across the Yukon River to Dawson City. The town is a cluster of mostly old buildings with many being refurbished. The only street that's paved is the main street which continues on to Whitehorse. All the rest of the streets are still dirt and today they were mud! We stopped along the Yukon, a park with picnic area and across the street was a variety of tourist shops. The area was well lighted and we felt safe…WRONG! A long haired native was appearing to look us over from his seat on the bench in front of us. Slowly with purpose, he turned his head around and looked back again. Jerry and I were sitting in the front seats of the van, it was dark and we had our inside light on. I turned it off and the glare of the street lights cast an eerie shadow across the park. The native got up and walked close to my side of the van, around the back and suddenly was tapping on Jerry's side window. Jerry started to roll it down and the native asked "what time is it? And that followed with a few foul words and threats of "I'm going to cut your throat", Jerry rolled the window up and we left the area and traveled a short distance to a campground. It makes us so mad that we can't stop where we want, only to be confronted by creeps like this. He appeared to be under the influence of some substance.

We are now at "Wolf Creek" a campground 12 miles east of Whitehorse. It is a beautiful primitive camp along a beautiful creek, which we are camped along side and can hear the rushing water. We had a beautiful drive today even in the rain.

WOLF CREEK

Tomorrow we'll drive the 396 miles to Laird Hot Springs (one of our favorite spots) to soak our bodies in the warm mineral waters.

August 29th, we are at Ft. Nelson and have left the mountains that we love so dearly. It is cool and raining now, but we had beautiful weather at Laird Hot Springs and we really enjoyed our time in the water. We left after another dip and a hearty breakfast to head for Muncho Lake. Took a stone in the windshield (our insurance company is going to love that). We had a windshield replaced the last two trips. We are 300 miles from Dawson Creek and once again already planning our return to our second home 'One More Time."

# FINAL RESTING PLACE

Alaska is among those places that some never leave and others like us return again and again which brings us to Chapter 4 in our continuing adventure.

It is May 6, 1991 and we are departing once again to our second home. Once again we leave from Florida, in our same van, with our same dog, Mandy. We had a wonderful send off from our friends with a tasty brunch and off we go.

We are now in Alabama, south of Montgomery and it is raining "cats and dogs." We didn't start this trip out real good. We had a flat tire at John and Donna's and the van was running a little warm. Two nights before we left, the house was broken into with strange things missing: a backpack, 2 fishing knifes, 1 flash light, can of WD40, can of tire inflator and a box of cookies. We had everything sitting out for our trip; video camera, 35 mm camera, TV, VCR, and briefcase with several thousand dollars of travelers checks, none of which were touched. Whoever it was even came into the bedroom and pulled out drawers, but never messed up anything. Police thought it was a young person. We've left our house year after year and never felt we had to worry. We refuse to let it spoil our trip and let the police handle it.

1pm and just south of Birmingham and stopped to get antifreeze to flush radiator and hope it runs cooler. It is 65 degrees, cloudy and windy. The trees here are freshly budded out, pretty light green and the fields are plowed with lots of water on them. We forget how beautiful spring can be and it's a reminder of how we miss the four seasons. Our lunch consists of peanut butter and jelly sandwiches and V8 juice. Far in the distance you can see the mountain range. The van is running cooler now. The flowers along the roadside are beautiful with an assortment of colors. There truly is so much to see and nature is so breathtaking.

Good morning! We are on Interstate 57 just north of Interstate 24 and headed for St. Louis, Missouri. We slept well. The van is running much better. We woke up to a temperature of about 48 degrees. Leaves are budded out here too and we wonder how far north before we find the bare trees. We stopped for a picnic lunch after coming through St. Louis. The city is a stark contrast of the old and new ways with each trying to survive. The city is a mixture of decaying concrete and steel. The "Gateway to the West" has all but been forgotten except for the striking arch to remind you. The fields are being plowed and the air smells fresh as we head west to Kansas City.

May 8th and BURR!! We woke up to cold weather and stayed at rest area on Interstate 90, just west of Sioux Falls, South Dakota. The temperature is 40 degrees. The landscape here is rolling hills, not many trees that give a stark, bare, cold feeling. It's very cloudy and windy. The fields here are freshly plowed and awaiting Mr. Winter to go away to enable planting of crops. We traveled 740 miles yesterday and do very well at keeping expenses around $50.00 a day (remember we are self contained and have all our own food).

I experienced a forgotten custom. I was on my way to the restroom building at a rest area and passed by a gentleman wearing a western hat, suit and boots and he "tipped" his hat and said, "Good day." It seemed like right out of a western movie. We are 250 miles east of Mt. Rushmore and we will enjoy filming this beautiful wonder that we had also visited in 1978. We are truly in Prairie Country and with imagination one can expect to see Indians over the next hill.

We continue west on Highway 90 and for as far as the eye can see, it is rolling high hills with no trees. The tumbleweed crosses the highway and stops at the fence line. Herds of cattle are seen in groups with cows nursing their calves. It's easy to see why these hills are called the "black hills"; the strong winds seem to strip all the top soil off leaving only the rich black soil visible. The landscape is painted with an occasional farm off in the distance.

May 9, we had many experiences yesterday, went back to Mr. Rushmore and filmed the great mountain, then on to "Crazy Horse" and were greatly disappointed as little progress had been made over the past 13 years. We continued our loop through the Black Hills and saw at least three to four hundred deer; during our 50 mile drive. Also saw our first snow in the valley. We came to a town nestled in the mountains called Deadwood. This has by far been the most unique town we've seen on this trip. Imagine if you can a 200 foot wide swath cut deep in the mountains, curving like a snake and fill it with a town and all the houses that are built up the mountain sides at every conceivable level and then add a bonus of "gambling in the town" and maybe you can get the picture. The town also looked straight out of the west with its olden days buildings (like *Gunsmoke*). It was almost dark when we came through, so all the buildings were lit up and you could see all the brightly colored slot machines through the windows. We resisted the temptation to stop or should I correct that to say…Jerry drove on through, knowing if he stopped, I'd still be there!

We drove on to the first rest area in Wyoming and fixed supper. As we sat later just talking, we had the privilege of seeing 2 deer feeding on the green leaves only 40 feet from us. We just sat and watched them for an hour or so. Finally, with full stomachs and a flick of their tail they were off into the night as just two of Gods Creatures…Free.

The landscape this morning is dotted with sagebrush, tumble weeds (no trees) and rolling hills and throw in literally hundreds of antelope. It is cooler now and patches of snow can be seen in the far distance. We have just sighted the majestic Teton Mountain Range and still approximately 200 miles away. One hundred miles east of Butte, Montana and we ran into a snow storm, everything is covered with snow, windy and very cold.

May 10th. Yesterday was another beautiful drive; we saw deer, antelope, wild turkeys and one dead fox and lots of snow. We stopped at a rest area about 60 miles east of Missoula, Montana. It was 33 degrees when we went to bed. We were toasty under our down filled comforter, even the dog was under the covers. We awoke to spitting snow and "cold, cold, cold!!

By 11am we were in Missoula and things were warming up a little, sun was out. Trees here are just budding out. Town is clean and nestled in the mountains. People hurrying around and us! We've slowed to a snail's pace and just enjoy each day. We're about 180 miles from our son's house and looking forward to a few days with him and his family.

We had another experience! We drove west on Interstate 90 to DeBorgia, Montana and expected to take a shortcut to Libby, Montana and US 2 and discovered the pass was all snowed in, so we had to back track 11 miles to another secondary road to cut through the mountains. We were told it was gravel, but wasn't told it was a "two track" and I do mean "2 tracks" for 50 to 60 miles. It was an adventure and somewhat scary when you think about breaking down clear out in the middle of nowhere. We saw a lot of deer and came upon a couple camping along the river. We looked a little foolish I think, when we asked "are we on the right road?" Jerry was in a short sleeved shirt and they were in snow mobile suits. They were very friendly and were hunting bear. We continued on our journey feeling like we were already in Alaska with rough roads, dust and miles and miles of wilderness. We met one truck on the whole trip so I guess that tells you that most people stick to the main roads.

We arrived back to civilization at 7 pm, some 40 miles from Libby, Montana (where our son lives). We drove on and found a motel to stop and clean up before our son and his family saw us. (Those spit baths only last so long).

May 13th. We spent the last 2 days with our son and family. We had a very special time with them and they really showed us around this beautiful area. They have a nice place on a creek. We parked by the creek and were lulled to sleep by the rushing waters with snow capped mountains in the background. We went for a hike in the mountains by a large waterfall. We had to walk on a swinging bridge to cross a gorge (approximately 200 feet across and 150 feet above the river), kind of made me weak in the knees. We took a lot of pictures and video. We ended our day with a steak cook out.

SWING BRIDGE OVER THE KOOTENAY RIVER

The next day we took a picnic lunch and headed up the mountains into grizzly habitat. There were signs posted regarding the bears and to our disappointment we didn't see any. We went "spike hunting" along the way and saw many medium size ones and then a lot of very big ones. Are you questioning what spike hunting is? Think about it for a while and I'll tell you later. We found a few areas on the mountain road partially blocked with snow, but the 4-wheel jeep went through with ease. About 6 miles into the trail, we encountered 2 feet of solid packed snow and ice and had to turn back. The day was raining and cold and we ended up eating in the jeep. On arriving home the guys took a nap and we took the girls to a movie.

Today we followed out to where our son and his partner are logging. A real unique experience, to say the least. Our son and his dog get ready to go up the mountain. His dog is a cross between a wolf and lab and he is a work dog during the day and a gentle family pet the rest of the time. He wears a back pack loaded with equipment needed to fall trees off the mountain side. I filmed the big trees as they fell and slid down the mountain with an echoing roar. We left the kids and plan to meet at Glacier National Park in the fall.

We continued north and entered Canada on Highway 97. We received the usual expected hassle at the border. They just tear apart the van looking for guns and it really ticks us off.

We simmered down about the border guards and now continue our climb into the Rockies of British Columbia. The landscape is green and white. Green pines and snow covered mountains which continue to get higher with each mile and we are about 140 miles south of Banff and will take in Kootenay, Yoho, Jasper and Banff National Parks. We exit Mt. Robinson (highest elevation in Canadian Rockies) 12,972 feet and then head west on Highway 16 to Prince George. The sun is out, but cold.

Yesterday will be remembered forever. We started the day with filming a pair of eagles and ended it with elk, but it was in between that is so special to us. We were traveling on Highway 93 in Jasper National Park when Jerry spotted a figure of what looked like a bear approximately ¾ mile away, high on the snow covered mountain. With our field glasses we could see clearly that it was a very large grizzly. It was so thrilling in as much as it's rare to site one in the wild (outside of observing them at McNeil River). We had stopped and filmed a 3 year old black bear who came within 10 feet from the van about 15 minutes prior to sighting this grizzly and that was nothing compared to the magnificent grizzly. Our biggest thrill was yet to come! We continued on our way about another ½ hour and came to an area where the slope of the mountain came right down to the road and there no more than 100 feet away was this beautiful grizzly eating grass. We backed up and I thought for sure it would leave and I wouldn't get a chance to film it, but not the case it just continued eating and we talked to it and finally he sat down and almost posed for me. He was huge, dark brown with touches of silver across his shoulders and back. We were shocked at the seemingly way we were being ignored by this beautiful creature. My guess is that they are very sluggish when they come out of hibernation and given a few days might respond different, we were excited about sighting 2 bears and a short time later sighted our 3rd one. This time the grizzly was down wind from us and when we got out of the van it started running along an open area with a stream between him and us.

All of this even surpassed the filming at McNeil River. Filming at McNeil is more of a "controlled area", where you know the bears are there feeding on salmon and they are more or less tolerant of the camera buffs.

THE BEAR

As it became dusk, we saw elk, one beaver and several deer. We parked outside the entrance to a camping area (not open yet). We awoke to wall-to-wall elk. They were all over and Mandy went wild. She wanted to go hunting.

ELK

We stopped for fuel in Jasper and headed northeast on Highway 16, headed for Grand Prairie and would you believe, we came upon a wolf. We sure have seen the wildlife. Exciting!!!

We spent the night in Ft. Nelson, drove some 600 miles yesterday from Jasper, Alberta. Weather is cold and sunny. Saw more wildlife, elk, reindeer, moose and deer. We will get some groceries here and start back into the Rockies. We've been mostly in valleys since leaving Jasper. We took another of Jerry's short cuts and it cost us 200 miles of gravel. Today we head west and southwest before turning north. This is a beautiful part of the trip; all mountains and perhaps a small settlement every 100 miles or so. When I say a settlement, I mean; gas station, groceries, restaurant, and cabins, more like a pony express stop. Oh yes!! Have you figured out what "Spike Hunting" is? Our son and his partner are logging in the Montana Mountains and they only cut the spike trees. They are the trees that look dead in the forest because their tops are bare and look like "spikes"

Imagine if you can, sitting by a nice camp fire in the mountains, sun still shinning through the pine and poplar trees and hear the "snap" of the wood as it burns as you sip on your evening toddy. That picture is us at Laird River Hot Springs. We arrived here about 3 pm and went for a dip in the hot springs as soon as camp was settled. Earlier in the day, Jerry had chased two moose around the gravel pit (with the van) and this was when we met Fred and Barbara Moehle from Massachusetts, who have been special friends ever since. We were walking to the hot springs with them, when a large moose came out of the marsh and stood right by the walkway. It was a stand off as to who had the right away. Jerry and Fred just kept walking and I will never forget the excitement in Barbara's voice when she said "not my husband, he isn't going to walk up to that thing." About that time the moose got right up on the walk way and crossed over as Barbara is screaming "I knew it, I knew he was going to do that." Fred and Barbara have been traveling since April 14, just visiting all parts of the country.

We sat around the fire till late and then went to bed around 10:45 (still light). This morning the weather is sunny and warm and the smell of fresh coffee outside is one of those treasured memories of camping. The birds are very busy providing music with our coffee. This is a very peaceful place.

May 17th and we start out early. First thing we saw was Mamma Moose and her yearling out for a walk. Sun is out and fairly warm. We want to drive to Wolf Creek (some 400 miles). Roads are getting rougher, lots of gravel and frost coming out of the ground. We are healthy, a few pounds heavier and enjoying every minute.

Just finished breakfast and so far we have seen 3 moose, lots of snowshoe rabbits and one ferret. We have fond thoughts of the past 2 days and our three different trips to soak in the hot springs. The area we're in now, (20 miles west of Watson Lake) is very dense, scrawny pine trees with snow capped mountains in the distance. It's colder with snow along sides of road and back in the high mountains where trees are taller and facilities few and far between.

8 pm and here we sit camped by Wolf Creek (12 miles east of Whitehorse). Our camp site is right on the rushing creek and we have a big fire going again. There are only a few camping in here. There is still snow to be seen on the mountain slopes that border this park. Tomorrow we will be back in the USA and will stay in Tok, Alaska and catch up on laundry and showers. Tok is 392 miles away. We came across miles and miles of bad roads today. Tomorrow we will stop at Whitehorse and get a few supplies.

We got another early start, sunny, but real cold. We left Wolf Creek and headed for Tok. We came across a herd of buffalo at Kluane Lake in Yukon Territory. We stopped and filled coolers with the most pure ice I've ever seen. We manage to avoid buying ice as much as possible. Our expenses have been averaging $55.00 per day and that includes every dime spent.

2:45 and just crossed into good old USA, the roads have been indescribable for the past 75 miles. It's sunny and warmer now; trees here are just starting to bud out. We feel as if we've gone through the 4 seasons in the past 16 days. The high Wrangell Mountains are to our left (all covered with snow) it's nice to read mileage signs in miles and not kilometers. Our destination is Tok and a shower.

5 pm arrived in Tok, got our camp site, nestled in the pines. It is warm out and we have the view of the Wrangells to the south. We ate out in the restaurant that everyone needs to stop at if ever in Tok. It is "Fast Eddy's Restaurant" and if you like breaded mushrooms, his can't be beat.

May 19th, another beautiful day. We are on our way to Anchorage, and approximately 160 miles more and we'll be there. At 2:40 pm the weather really took a switch. We are in a snow storm! And this area is very mountainous with switch backs and high elevations. We also are following Fred and Barb, and right now they are probably wishing they hadn't listened to us urging them to come to Homer. They had only intended to go as far as Haines Junction and turn around. We plan on camping about 60 miles up the road. The roads are getting very slippery. We reached King Mountain State Park and found a camp site. The park is on the Matanuska River. The color of the river is milky white from the glacier run off. It was one of our coldest nights.

We finally arrived in Anchorage on May 20th and went for a relaxing dinner before turning in for the night. The next morning we went for supplies for our time in

Homer. It was such a bright and clear day that we were able to film Mt. McKinley (150 miles away), a magnificent sight to see. We headed south and we were still on the expressway, when we spotted a bull moose walking along the fence line looking bewildered and being trapped between the highway and the fence. It's very common to see moose in town.

Our next big sighting was when we were traveling along Turnagain Arm, there were 6 Killer Whales trapped in the low tide. It was a sight to behold and hope they make it out when the tide comes back up. It was sad to see them thrash about and feeling helpless in not being able to do anything.

May 23rd, the whales made it out safely. We are finally settled in after doing all the work it takes to open a trailer after 9 months. The weather has been unseasonably beautiful and we are about ready to leave for King Salmon fishing.

This year I will be working in the Emergency Department of Central Peninsula General Hospital, in Soldotna, which is about 75 miles north of here. The staffing at South Peninsula Hospital, here in Homer is adequate for this summer. I will be working every Friday, Saturday and Sunday 11 am to 11 pm. The ER is beautiful and they have the latest equipment, so I'm ready for the next challenge.

May 24th, no kings were caught, so we went hooligan fishing and no luck there either; guess we just need to get warmed up to the fishing again! We still have beautiful weather 55 to 60 degrees during the day and low 40 at night. We have had one moose in camp so far. The trailer is in the same spot, so once again we view the bay and glaciers from our windows. Today we saw a school of pilot whales in Cook Inlet. Fred and Barbara made it to Homer and are camped on the Spit.

We went to Tom and Jeans for halibut last night, oh so good!! Then we filmed a moose with her newborn twins that Tom and Jean had seen born the night before and it never ceases to thrill me year after year to see such an event. Today was work day for us; we hauled water for the entire camp. It took us 4 hours to haul 1000 gallons, but now everyone can take showers. Then it was on to the Laundromat for us. It's funny, if we had to do all these things other than by choice, we would resent it for sure. Tomorrow is the annual Memorial Day picnic at Tom and Jean's. They always have Cotton Moore come with his BBQ wagon and he does the best chicken and ribs you would ever want to eat.

COTTON MOORE

Jackie is also back in Homer, after spending the winter in Florida. She seems to be doing ok, but I'm sure it's difficult to come back to the memories of living in Alaska for so long, without Bud.

May 27th and Happy Memorial Day! We had our ribs and chicken, the weather didn't cooperate though, it was cold and rainy and 40 degrees. We could have used just a little of the Florida temperatures.

A busy day! Jerry went fishing at 3:30 am and got his first King Salmon of the season. The salmon weighed 16 pounds and he will smoke it tomorrow.

'RED' THE PROUD FISHERMAN

I stayed in bed, still getting over an ear infection, but other wise ok. We went down to the Spit later and saw the seals in the fishing hole who were competing with the fisherman. It is cold and raining again. Mr. Moose visited camp again and Jackie left for Anchorage today. We have made a decision to buy the 5$^{th}$ wheel from Jackie and just leave it here as always.

Went fishing at the fishing hole, and no luck; so disgusting to see them swim by your hook. Jerry smoked his fish and it was absolutely delicious. Still cold and raining and you can hardly see the mountains with all the clouds. We are snug and warm in our trailer and tomorrow leave for Soldotna and will camp at Kasilof State Park with our van and a 12 by 12 screen room (should be interesting), but rent in Soldotna is out of the question, and we will only be there 3 nights a week.

The camp site is set up and we are right on the river, we set up the screen room (after a few laughs) and then had ribs and left over boiled dinner for supper. The weather has cleared a little and the park is full as everyone has "King Salmon

Fever". We went to Crooked Creek and it was "combat fishing" at its best (shoulder to shoulder) and that park was full too. It is 11 pm and bright as day out. This roughing it will be the final test of togetherness and if we do this, we have surely passed the survival test. Tomorrow is another day! As Jerry puts it; our king size bed is down to a twin size bed. The weather at night is so cold; we have a "night cap" to keep antifreeze in our blood.

Well! I made it through the first shift at the new hospital, busy place and the nurses do everything. There is only one RN on duty per shift and one ER tech and tonight they saw 28 patients. The hardest part of a new job is the massive amount of paper work, and here they have twice as much as we do in Florida. The frustrating part is that there is very little time left for patient care.

Back in Homer and will catch up on what has been happening over the past 3 days. We survived our first camp out and work. We truly feel we could survive in the wilderness on next to nothing if need be. Work went well, staff is great and I had already worked with some of the same physicians in Homer. My orientation lasted about 1 hour! And then it was "your on your own", oh well, busy place, but shift goes fast. I'm working 12 hour shifts and will work a couple of night shifts, which will prove interesting as I am not a night person. Jerry and I joke about listing the van for sale in the following manner "one small motor home completely equipped...for midgets" but we do well with sitting up our screen room around the picnic table and that gives us more room in the van being that a lot of items can be in the screen room. Jerry took me to work and then he had the awful duty to "fish all day", something is wrong with this picture. We are really enjoying this latest experience, but it sure was nice to get back to Homer, where we could stand upright, shower and have TV, phone and all those things that we take for granted. The experience really makes you appreciate everything you have and gives a whole new perspective on life.

This morning, Mother Moose and her baby came walking down our drive. What a sight! Today is cold...38 degrees, raining but a good day for laundry and other chores. We will be here till Thursday morning and then back to Soldotna for work Thursday, Friday and then 6 days off.

We've been gone from home for 1 month and really it seems like much longer. Jerry is fishing today and I'm brushing up for a pharmacy exam which is required for all new hire nurses. The town is busy with all the tourists. The post office and grocery store traffic remind me of Pine Island, Florida in the winter.

Catch up time again! We are back in Homer, pharmacy test was a bummer! Geared mostly for floor nursing, but managed to get through it (not with flying colors though), but otherwise we spent our morning at the camp site relaxing and then off to work for me and fishing for Jerry (he has it made).

Yesterday was a special, but sad day for us. We had a memorial for Bud as he had requested. Three commercial fishing vessels took a group of people, consisting of family and friends out to sea in Cook Inlet and then took smaller skiffs to shore where a beautiful service was held. We laid fresh flowers on the rocky beach and after a beautiful verbal tribute; his ashes were sprinkled in the wind for his "FINAL RESTING PLACE' on the beach, until the tides came up to wash the ashes out to sea. After the service we all went back to the big boats and spent several hours fishing for halibut. We completed the day with a picnic back at camp. All of this was Bud's wishes and we all felt his presence. We miss him a lot.

Today we went out fishing again for halibut. We are fortunate to have friends that have a commercial boat and to be able to get out sea often. The boat is 44 feet and will only be in port for another couple of weeks before heading out for salmon fishing for the balance of June, July and August. Between the six of us, there were 5 halibut, 3 flounder and 1 ling cod caught. The weather has been beautiful the past 2 days. It's been a long day on the water and were all going to Don Jose's for margaritas and nachos.

June 10th and Jerry is smoking fish and I'm about ready to do the awful task of laundry. Tomorrow we head up the bay to get butter clams. Last night we had Tanner crabs. You can see we are starving.

Up early to catch the low tides and go up the bay about 20 miles. We pulled the skiff behind the big boat and then went ashore in it. To get the tasty morsels you watch where they are spurting water and then rake in that spot. Bottom line is we got our fill of pail after pail and then went up the beach more to get "black mussels" After that we continued up the bay to "Bear Cove", a beautiful primitive cove with a few cabins that can only be reached by boat or plane. We then came home to rest after the successful day.

We were sitting in the 5<sup>th</sup> wheel at 5:23 pm and the trailer shook hard for approximately 1 minute. We had an earthquake of 5.3 on the Richter Scale. Hope we don't have any more of that! We all got together for a clam feast and pigged out.

Another beautiful day and hope to fish for kings and must plan for going back to Soldotna tomorrow as I work the next three days.

June 17th, and catch up time. The last 3 days at work was a nightmare and we left to drive back to Homer at midnight after the 3rd day. We headed south to Ninilchek, where we spent the night. We saw about a dozen moose, including a very large bull. This morning we are parked at the Russian village of Ninilchek. This is a small quaint village by the sea with a channel coming into the harbor and this is where everyone is fishing for the famed king salmon. This is the last day for fishing kings here for the season. High up on a hill overlooking the village and harbor is a Russian Church which seems to act as a sentinel for the fisherman and a symbol of a higher being looking out for all.

We are sitting by the sea watching the tide go out and there are 3 eagles on the beach waiting for clams. Several people are out trying their luck to dig for razor clams (a lot of hard work) and the clam usually is faster than you.

This day was a poor day for fishing. Jerry got 2 on and I had one and we lost all 3. My struggle with the big fish left me very wet and muddy. When my fish hit, I didn't realize that my feet were mired in glacier mud, and when the fish took off, I couldn't move and promptly took my seat in the water trying to hold on to the fish which threw the hook and I was not left "high and dry". We spent 24 hours there and finally gave up at 1am and headed for Homer. We had to slam the breaks to avoid a head on collision with Mrs. Moose and that shifted a few things around in the van! We also saw a black bear cub on the side of the road and decided not to push our luck to investigate it further, as mother bear was sure to be close by.

Jackie is leaving here June 29th for Michigan and then back to Florida the first of August. Not really sure, but feel that it is difficult for Jackie to be here with so many memories. We will move into Jackie's trailer and what a change for us from a 28 foot 5th wheel to a 70 foot mobile home and we're ready for some room. We will winterize the 5th wheel and do the same to the mobile before leaving here in September. It was so generous of Jackie and we sure appreciate it. It will also make it so much easier when our daughter, son-in-law and grandson arrive in August.

June 22nd, and here we sit high on a hill overlooking the Kenai River. The weather is beautiful as we sit at the picnic table having coffee. I worked 7P to 7A last night and know for sure those hours are not for me. I have two more of those shifts and then back to the 11A to 11P schedule.

The birds are singing and this campground is filling up. We took a walk down to the river and the sockeye salmon are starting to run. This is a State Park (Morgan's Landing) which is about 80 miles north of Homer. The wild flowers are plentiful and the ferns are not trampled down yet; give another few days and this area will be over run with fishermen and fisherwomen!

Back in Homer and I'm still disoriented to which is day or night. It really affects me to switch from PM to Nights; maybe if you did it all the time, it would be ok. I can't believe that next week will be July! And the middle of July will be half point for us and then 2 ½ more months and we will be back at home.

Our friends, Walt and Dot arrived in Homer a couple of days ago (from Pine Island), and we spent a most enjoyable day with them. They will leave here Friday and follow us down to Soldotna and camp at Morgan's Landing for the weekend.

July 3rd and I have a lot of catching up! Walt and Dot are back in Homer, we all went to Morgan's Landing and camped for four days. I worked the weekend while they fished for sockeye salmon on the Russian River. Friday night Jerry picked me up at 11:45 pm from work and went back to camp for fresh salmon steaks over an open pit fire (it was still light out). On Monday I got to go fishing too! I wasn't in the river 30 minutes, when I lost my balance and down I went…FREEZING COLD, but being the true fisherwoman that I am I stood back up and fished for several hours more until I had uncontrollable shivering and had to stop and NO FISH!! The guys caught a total of 15 fish over the 4 days and we went back to Homer. Walt and Dot decided to come back to Homer for a couple more weeks.

WALT AND DOT PACKING THEIR SALMON IN JARS

We are now in Jackie's trailer, which is a 14 by 70 mobile with an expando living room, so needless to say we are enjoying the space. We had Walt and Dot over for a clam feast. Tomorrow we celebrate the 4th at the annual Elks Club Picnic. Friday we will leave for Morgan's Landing again in hopes of a more successful salmon run.

We had another close call with a moose/van collision. The moose ran out of the woods headed for the passenger side of the van and at the last minute the moose put his brakes on! Thank goodness. We get at least 2 accidents a week from auto/moose connection. We talked with Jackie last night, she said Michigan weather was hot, but she was really having a good time with her family.

July 16th and we are still between good and bad fishing. The sockeye are late in their return from the ocean, so we camped at Morgan's once again with all the others waiting for the fish. I worked 4 days in a row for a total of 44 hours and was dead on my feet. I'm really looking forward to my time off when our daughter and her family arrive from Michigan.

Weather here has been lousy, rain, rain and more rain. Dot and Walt are still here and we sure enjoy their company. They are camped at Johnson's Lake (about 60 miles north of Homer)

We spent last weekend at Morgan's, nice weather, packed campground and all waiting for sockeye. The fish started coming in although very slow. Walt and Dot left yesterday for Anchorage and to continue on with their travels; we will miss them and treasure their visit here. My last 3 days will be this weekend at Soldotna and then our daughter; Carla and her husband, Stan, and grandson Jason will arrive for a 2 week stay (can hardly wait). I have also been doing some PRN work here at Homer and will continue to do that until the last 2 weeks in August. I really could work 7 days a week, but no thanks. I sure have been doing a lot of pediatrics and I'll be glad to get back to the "elderly population" (ha ha). Today I am working ICU at Homer, going to work a few extra shifts to make up for my spending when our kids get here, also "lizzy" the van is in the shop for a valve job, I guess she figured three years of trucking us back and forth, called for a overhaul.

Jackie called and will be heading back to Florida soon. As for us, we enjoy the low temperature here, but could stand a little less rain. I look out my window and see a different picture each day with the sun and clouds casting different shadows on the glaciers and the bay. Last week I filmed an eagle on the stony beach, I walked up to within 20 feet (not to smart) and what an experience, they are so beautiful and so big. Next Thursday we pick up the tent camper trailer that we rented for the kids and drive up to Morgan's Landing, set up camp and then leave from there on Friday for Anchorage to pick them up at the airport. We will stay in Anchorage Friday night and then get supplies on Saturday and head back down to Morgan's Landing to spend 3 to 4 days fishing and then on to Homer for the rest of the time.

July 24th, busy night in Homer Hospital. There were no patients in ICU, so I worked the floor and not fun! I really have an appreciation for floor nurses and if I had to do it all the time, I'd get out of nursing. Our excitement for the day is a trip to the post office, bank and check on lizzy, haul water and go out for dinner with Jean. The ship "Green Peace" is in port this week.

What a beautiful day! The glaciers just glisten and temperature is 52 degrees. I'll take this day to make a video for Donna's mom (for her birthday). We are all packed and tomorrow we pick up the tent camper and head for Morgan's Landing. Last week they closed the river to fishing for sockeye and I thought we'd had part of our time with the kids ruined for sure, but the river was opened again last Monday. I never have seen so many fish; you could walk across the river on fish! Jerry got 4 and I didn't manage to land any.

We made our trip to Anchorage to pick up our kids and spent the night in Anchorage before heading back down to Morgan's. We had pulled the tent camper from Homer to Morgan's with no problems and set up camp. When we headed down the Kenai Peninsula, we stopped at all the usual tourist places; we went hiking at McHugh Creek, just south of Anchorage. The trail there is frequented by a lot of hikers. Four days after we had hiked there, an elderly woman, her son and grandson were attacked by a grizzly on the same trail that we had been on. The woman and her son were both killed and the grandson survived by climbing a tree. Grizzly bears are not good tree climbers. We also hiked an area of flats and glaciers, which was absolutely beautiful.

CARLA ON THE HIKING TRAIL

We even managed to sight a few wildlife enroute.

DOLL SHEEP, YOU ARE IN MY ROAD

Monday we went to the Russian River and what a time we had. The Russian and the Kenai River conjoin here and you must take a ferry across a 200 foot span of water to fish on the other side. Jerry and Stan really got into it. Stan hooked into a 50 pound king, which dragged him down stream before breaking the line.

STAN AND HIS KING SALMON

JASON'S TURN

CAMP SITE AT MORGAN'S  ~  DINNER ON THE GRILL

HAULING THE FISH

We came home with 10 sockeye and the weather was good for a change. On Tuesday we packed up and headed for Homer. We were all glad to have a shower and then met Jean at Jose's for happy hour. We ended the night with watching the video of our travels and eating blackened salmon....so good!

A beautiful day again... Carla and Stan are out for a walk, Jason's sleeping in (he went to a movie last night). Today we are going to head up the mountain that overlooks the village to view and take pictures. We also will have a picnic, and tomorrow we need to can our fish.

STAN CLEANING HIS FISH

RED  GETTING THE CANNER READY

Today we are going to dig for razor clams, which is sure to be an experience that Stan, Carla and Jason won't soon forget.

DIGGING IN THE MUD FOR RAZOR CLAMS

Back at camp in Homer, and Carla wasn't exactly sure she wanted to clean the clams, but in order to eat, you have to clean.

NOT THE CLEANEST JOB IN THE WORLD

Tom and Jean came to everyone's rescue by going out for a day of halibut fishing and then over to Halibut Cove for lunch.

A GOOD CATCH OF HALIBUT

LUNCH AT HALIBUT COVE

August 15<sup>th</sup> and the kids are back home and I miss them already. We had a great visit and were able to do everything we had planned. The weather cooperated and started to rain when they flew out and is still dark and raining. They got a touch of catching fish, digging up clams, picking berries and rhubarb and then cooking, canning and smoking and of course eating! At one point Carla stated "Mom, don't you ever buy food from the store any more?"

Now its work for us to get the trailer winterized when we leave, which is only a couple of weeks. I am only signed up for pool here in Homer and have enjoyed my time off.

August 25<sup>th</sup>, we said our goodbyes to everyone and looked back on our little Alaska home as we drove out the drive. We both look forward to coming home, but also will miss Homer. It was a little easier to leave though in view of the very windy, cold and rain, rain and more rain. We will drive to Soldotna tonight and then on to Anchorage tomorrow.

It got down to 37 last night. We ended up in a mall parking lot next to McDonalds, convenient right? Sun is trying to shine in between what looks like "snow" clouds. One could see their breath this morning. So it is time to leave.

The mountains here have already gotten their first dusting of snow and the trees are all varied hues of yellow.

We stayed in Tok last night (very cold) and started out at 8:30 am. We are now on the "Top of the World Highway" again and heading for the direction of the Artic Circle. We decided to go this route one more time in hopes of seeing the ten's of thousands of caribou as they migrate through here to the south. We have been winding around through the remnants of the old gold mines and then back up the mountains with the sharp switch backs. Most of the time, we are above the clouds. Eventually we will be above the tree line with nothing but tundra. The history here is mind jolting as we come across what's left of an old cabin by a rushing stream and wish we could relive for a moment the days back then.

August 29<sup>th</sup> and we are in Dawson City. We went to Diamond Tooth Gerties, a review and gambling palace. I easily gave my $50.00. A guy next to me won

$1800.00 on a machine that Jerry had been playing ...oh well!! Now on to Whitehorse.

August 30th and here we sit at our favorite spot, Laird Hot Springs. We have a roaring fire; have already soaked in the springs. Jerry is preparing the steaks ($15.98/kg). It's warmer here and we will stay here for 2 or 3 nights and enjoy the peacefulness. They have posted additional "Bear Danger" signs, so we'll be on the watch. We have met so many people who have taken the journey north to Alaska. Like us, they are returning to their homes somewhere in the lower 48.

On the road again, must be us! The hot springs area had been dry all summer till we arrived!! It rained all night and we barely managed to get breakfast cooked in between rain drops. The park rangers had to kill a bear in camp last night, after it chased a mom and her 3 kids off the boardwalk to the spring's area. Some other campers came by and told us a bear was on the next site to ours (as I was cooking bacon), I was already to film Jerry sharing his breakfast with Mr. Bear, but never did see it.

These last 3 days have been a nightmare. Our dog, Mandy got real sick 5 days ago and we thought it was car sickness, but then her breathing became fast and labored and 2 days ago we took her to a vet in Whitehorse and she was in pulmonary edema, probably secondary to a heart attack and/or congestive failure. The vet was great and did an EKG, X-RAY and started her on Lanoxin and Lasix and stated that he didn't think she would make it much longer. He told us there was a medical doctor in Ft. Nelson who would put her to sleep if needed.

September 5th and Mandy is doing much better, isn't eating but we are force feeding her. Jerry and I are not getting much sleep as she has to get up often to pee due to the lasix. We are just hoping to get her back home.

It is time to end this chapter of our adventure and to continue again hopefully "One More Time."

# RETURN TO HOMER

May 4, 1992 and once again we are still traveling in our same van (hopefully it will get us there and back). We are especially saddened to leave our little Mandy behind. She died on April 16th and somehow the crew in the van seems incomplete, but we have a picture of her and she will always be in our hearts.

MANDY

As we drive down Interstate 75 we are once again blessed with the roadside flowers; yellow, purple and white. The traffic is heavy and it is very warm as we leave from Florida. Again we have packed too much and could survive for at least a month if we get snowed in.

We just turned off 75 on to 50 west to Brooksville and still very warm and humid. The oak trees are so beautiful with moss hanging to the ground and every thing here is so green.

Day 2 and Jerry drove on till 1:30 am. We slept in a rest area north of Montgomery, Alabama; it is a beautiful cool and crisp morning. It really looks like spring here, with new green, lush foliage. We are coming into Birmingham, Alabama and the sky is a sea of pollution. We may not have industry and high paying jobs in Florida, but we do have clear skies.

The country side is beautiful as we wind our way through the hills, now you can see rock formations as the hills slope away from the highway. We are starting to see buds on the trees and it's like a reversal of spring as we continue north.

Our weather has turned cloudy and cool, we've had lunch and we are about 25 miles south of Nashville, Tennessee. Off in the distance you can see mountains and there is heavy rain that we appear headed for, as all the vehicles headed our way have their lights on.

We are just coming into St. Louis, Missouri. The land has flattened out again and the farmers seem to be in high gear, sometimes against the elements. St. Louis is a big city, sprawled out for 25 miles or more. The city itself holds ones curiosity as to the memories it holds. A mix of new and old with the reminders of the different eras it has gone through. Its history as a cattle town and "Gateway to the West" leaves us with questions as we travel along the river and see the decaying buildings that once represented the giant industry of steel mills; now departed to a new trend of building outside the cities. It's sad at best, that we so quickly tend to forget the old in favor of the new, when it is the old that gives us our heritage, history and support system with all of its memories.

We stopped at a rest area and ate supper, this time it was the southern fried chicken that I did before leaving Florida. All the rest of our prepared food is frozen, so starting tomorrow we will vary our diet a little. We continued on and the van heater feels good. We have the most beautiful sunset as we continue on to the west.

May 6th, we drove 715 miles yesterday. It is very cold this morning, but making the coffee took the chill out of the van and us too. It is bight and sunny but cold. The landscape looks like a patchwork quilt. This is farmer's country and it is getting flatter. We are 50 miles east of Kansas City, Missouri.

11:30 and we are now on Interstate 29 going north towards Council Bluff, Iowa. The remnants of winter remain here with the dead grass matted down from heavy snow and although the snow is gone, spring is slow to arrive. Some of the trees are bare yet and everything looks grey. It's strange that we're going north and we've heard that it is warmer up ahead.

We are just south of Sioux City, Iowa. The landscape remains flat and the only trees you see are the ones that surround the occasional farm houses that dot the landscape as we follow the Mississippi River. I sit here day dreaming about what it would be like to live on one of these farms.

May 7$^{th}$ and imagine if you can, a rest area nestled in a ravine surrounded by the foothills of the "Bad Lands" in South Dakota, it is absolutely a beautiful morning, sunny, warm with an expected high in the 80s. There is a gentle breeze and the birds seem to be competing in song. I'm setting at a picnic table; coffee is brewing on our portable stove and what more could we ask for? We are going to stop at the "Las Vegas" type town of "Deadwood", which is about 60 miles west of here and I'm sure we will contribute our money like all the other gambling fools.

We just got our first glimpse of the Black Hills of South Dakota as we continue our journey west on highway 90. We're about 25 miles east of Rapid City and we've come 2000 miles in less than 3 days. Now we will slow down a bit, because the country gets more beautiful with each mile. Last year we came through a snow storm in this area and today it is in the 70s.

4:45 pm and it's like I said, we contributed to the town of "Deadwood", $145.00 to be exact. We got free (ha), 2 coffees, 1 coke and about 4 beers and 5 hours later we left. It was really fun though! So if you figure it out the drinks cost us an average of $13.18 each. We are now headed west again and now we are in Wyoming and you wouldn't believe how hot it is here....95 degrees and probably warmer than Ft. Myers, Florida.

The terrain is rolling hills with cattle grazing and no trees in sight, just sage brush. You can see a farm about once every 5 miles, the soil is red.

Just got our first glimpse of the Teton Mountains, they are so beautiful and truly a sight to behold.

May 8. Imagine if you can, waking up to a beautiful morning, birds singing, no wind and off in the distance the snow capped Rockies. We are in a rest area high on a hill overlooking the valley with a river winding through. We are west of Billings, Montana and headed for Missoula, Montana where it's time for a motel. We saw the usual hundreds of antelope and mule deer while driving through Wyoming. From here on the trip is nothing but beauty.

11:30 am, and we are east of Butte, Montana. It has turned cold and we are deep in the mountains. These mountains look like they exploded at one time and all came down as rocks of every shape. We continue to climb to get over one summit after another. We are going to stay at Lakeside Resort tonight on Highway 93 northwest of Missoula, Montana.

2:15 pm and now headed north through canyons on Highway 93 to Kalispell, Montana. It is sunny out and warm with just the peaks having snow on. We have yet to come through a snow storm (a first so far). We are traveling through "Flathead Indian Reservation", and we are in a valley and the landscape is dotted with neat small ranches and lots of horses. The trees are just budding out and lilacs are in bloom.

We finally made our destination for the day and we are in a beautiful motel with all the creature comforts. Its funny how we take things for granted until we don't have them. We are 90 miles from our son's home.

On the road again. It is cool and raining as we wind through the mountains on US 2, heading west to Libby, Montana. Jerry won $11.00 on the slot machine last night (not me!!). The hotel we stayed at was Diamond Lils, and who could resist the temptation?

May 11th. We spent the last two days with our son and his family. The girls have sure grown and they moved into a bigger house. We went out for Mother's Day Dinner and spent time playing cards as weather didn't cooperate. We just came through Bonners Ferry, Idaho and now on a different time zone again (went back an hour). We are headed now for the Canadian border, deep in the mountains with the Moyie River winding along side. We wonder if customs will tear us apart again this year. This year we are traveling with a shotgun due to our feeling unsafe with the two bad experiences that we have had.

Customs never looked in the van, this year they were in to checking on alcohol and we ended up paying $12.00 US dollars for exceeding our limit. They asked about guns, but never asked to see it when we told them we had one. (Hard to figure).

We are now about 30 miles from the entrance into Jasper National Park. The Canadian Rockies are among the most beautiful mountains in the world. The mountains continue to be higher and higher, and with more snow the further north we go.

2:45 pm, at Radium Hot Springs, this is a commercial attraction built around a natural springs.

RADIUM HOT SPRINGS

As we entered the hot springs area, we came into a terrific snow storm, with accumulation on the road, and it turned very cold. This is where you enter the four national parks on approximately a 150 mile drive through absolute beauty.

May 12th. We spent our coldest night ever on this trip, we were warm under the comforter, but you didn't dare venture out. We must have intruded on coyote territory, because they howled to us during the night. We woke up to everything covered with frost, but it's absolutely beautiful, sunny and crisp. We have already seen a dozen or so elk, 2 coyote and several mountain sheep. The lower altitudes of the mountain slopes are all dusted with fresh new snow.

It is 9 am and we are on Highway 40 north to Grand Prairie, Alberta. This stretch of road is 180 miles long with a town at the 80 mile marker and 120 of the miles are gravel. It remains extremely cold with snow at the road level and our destination today is Fort Nelson, British Columbia.

4:20 pm. at Fort St. John on the Alaska Highway. We are at a car wash to get the mud off the van. Just took on some supplies for the next leg of our journey. Get these prices: 2 small T-bone steaks, 4 potatoes, 2 onions, loaf of bread, quart of milk, eggs and bacon=$37.70….cheap right?

6 pm, 160 miles east of Fort Nelson. It is getting very cold again and snow is covering the road now. We have never made this trip with so much snow and hope this isn't a sign of what summer is going to be like.

May 13th, camped out again and woke to a cloudy, cold morning. We are heading for the summit (highest point on the Alaskan Highway). We have seen 2 moose, snowshoe rabbit, quail and 1 reindeer. We have come 442 miles west from Dawson Creek and it's still snowing.

We finally stopped for the night and imagine if you can, us sitting around the camp fire, big old chunk of tree for our end table and we have just come back from our soak in Laird Hot Springs and we feel refreshed! Once again we are at one of our favorite stops.

This is always such a relaxing stop for us. We will stay here for a couple of days. The temperature is about 55 degrees and we've never been here when spring has been so late. The buds are barely forming. The camp is filling up fast as it is a well know "way stop" for weary travelers.

We slept in till 9 am, had coffee and went for a morning soak and visited with other travelers, came back to camp and fixed breakfast outside in the crisp, but sunny morning. We have been out now for 11 days and love every minute. It's so peaceful to sit around the camp fire and just relax.

May 15th, we left Laird after truly relaxing and enjoying the springs and look forward to stopping there on the way back home. Everyone who makes this trip must put Laird as one of their "must stop list". Everything was covered with frost this morning. It is sunny, but cold. Still quite an accumulation of snow as we meander around the mountains. We have seen a black bear this morning and also saw one on the way back from the spring last night. We ran into friends of ours that we have seen each year for the last 3 years. They are from Texas, Bill and Maxine Spencer, they have managed the campground at Morgan's for the past three years and this summer they are spending it on Kodiak Island.

Just came into Yukon Territory and coming into Watson Lake. We have seen 2 more black bears, but one was dead on the road (apparently hit by a car). The Alaskan Highway is a better road now, straighter and mostly paved, but the animals suffer more due to the increased speed of the travelers. We remember back in 1984 when the top speed was 45 miles an hour in most places. Now you see drivers exceeding the speed limits. We liked the road better when it was more of a challenge to wind in and around the mountains and you had more of a chance to view animals with a slower speed.

We stopped at the junction of the Alaska Highway and 37 (the Cassiar Highway) for coffee and shared one big cinnamon roll (6"X 6"). There is snow all over and very cold.

The road is especially bad and we are stopped waiting for a truck to clear. We are on broken pavement and mud where other trucks are pushing the truck clear. We are approximately 135 miles east of Whitehorse. Weather report is still the same! Cold and lots of snow. The picnic tables in the picnic area were covered with snow, so needless to say we ate in the van.

We finally reached Whitehorse, and Pioneer Campground. Just finished with showers and have two loads of laundry to do. It is colder than !!#**!! here. The park just opened yesterday. Jerry called his friend, Hank Carr, whom we met a couple of years ago. Hank is a local singer/entertainer in Whitehorse and we will go and listen to him play at one of the local pubs tonight.

We had interesting visit with a couple from Ft. Myers, Florida and also saw our friends from Texas again as they are camped here too.

May 16th. Seems more like February! We woke up to 4 inches of snow.

SNOW IN WHITEHORSE

We had to use our spatula to get ice and snow off windows. It really is a different year. We leave for Tok this AM, approximately 400 miles away. Oh yes! Please send money. We each had 2 drinks last night while listening to Hank play and they came to $14.80. and that was draft beer. ($3.70 each beer), needless to say we sipped slowly.

12:45 pm, we stopped and fixed breakfast in the van, we just came through Haines Junction and even though there is a lot of snow, it is sunny now and clear and the mountains are absolutely majestic. Two grey wolves ran out in front of us earlier. By 1:30 the ice and snow melted off the van and now we are going around Kluane Lake. The road is rough and the lake is frozen over.

3 pm and I know everyone is tired of hearing this, but it is snowing again! It snows so hard at times it is a white out. We are on some of our worst roads for the next 100 miles. Remember when I said we had enough food for a month? Well we may need it if we get snowed in. This really isn't what we had in mind. I remember

saying I'd like to travel to Alaska in the winter. Well I wish all my other wishes would come true (please send warm weather).

5:15 pm and finally got to the Alaska border...36 degrees out (heat wave) and really the weather has improved, a lot less snow, but still all the lakes are frozen over. The custom guys said last month was warmer.

10:20 pm and picture if you can, us following a huge moose down the highway! Yes following! The moose had been on the shoulder of the road when we first saw it, so we slowed down and then the critter came down and proceeded to walk down the road directly in front of us for quite a few minutes. The roads were covered with snow and it was a bright clear night, so it was quite a picture captured with the video camera.

May 17th, woke up to a beautiful, sunny morning (can't believe it). We slept in a State Park Campground, which was not open yet officially, so no fee. So far we have paid for 3 nights camping and 1 night in a motel. Tonight we will be in Anchorage and then on to Homer.

May 19th, spent 2 days in Anchorage, resting and stocking up with supplies and now we are headed down the Kenai Peninsula to Homer. The drive is famous for being one of the most beautiful scenic drives in the world. The temperature is 57 degrees and sunny. This drive is 240 miles from Anchorage to Homer and takes you by breathtaking scenery. You will see Cook Inlet, Turnagain Arm, Portage Glacier, and volcanoes, the world famous Russian and Kenai Rivers along with quaint little villages and towns.

We finally arrived in Homer and spent the last 2 days getting unpacked and organized and now we're ready to go halibut fishing. It has been sunny and nice so we took advantage of it and washed the 5th wheel.

Went king salmon fishing today and no luck. I think all of Anchorage is on the Kenai Peninsula this weekend. On the 25th, we went to Tom and Jean's annual Memorial Day picnic and Cotton Moore did his wonderful BBQ ribs and delicious chicken. I think everyone overate, I know I did. Tomorrow back to fishing again and on Wednesday I go back to my summer job at the hospital here.

I spent several hours at the hospital today, with required orientation of safety, fire and body mechanics. I've decided to go pool rather then a definite schedule, that way I can work when I want to! I really don't want to work more than a couple of shifts per week (heard that before?) I need more time for fishing. The weather has been great and we spent time cleaning brush from around the 5<sup>th</sup> wheel. Mrs. Moose was in camp twice today, but no babies seen.

May 28<sup>th</sup> and finally moose babies, 2 of them and when we saw them, their legs were wobbly and what a sight.

Just got home after working the 3 to 11 shift, it was really great to see old friends and didn't take long to feel back at home. Came home and had to come to complete stop just before our drive, there was a baby moose in the road and it finally got mamma's message to get out of the road and it ran back to mom. I'm working tomorrow and the next day. (So much for a couple of shifts per week). They are so short staffed and it is hard for me to say no.

May 30<sup>th</sup> and Jerry caught his first salmon of this season and will smoke it tomorrow. Jerry learned his smoking technique and recipe from Bud and will always be reminded of Bud every time he smokes. Jerry had another one on, but it stripped his new reel. I lost both of the salmon that I had on.

Another day and Jerry has gone fishing again, as for me, I have a sore throat, headache and ache all over. I'm also getting cabin fever. The weather has been great and here I sit. I have been doctoring myself and guess maybe I should see a real doctor. I'm not a good patient either (most nurses are not).

Today we're going across the bay to the village of Seldovia a quaint fishing village and long ago were the social and economic heart of the lower Cook Inlet. It was also one of Alaska's busiest seaports. Boats carried mail and supplies to Homer from Seldovia. There are only a few hundred year-round residents in Seldovia, which can only be reached by boat or plane.

Our friend Jackie is starting to pack for her trip back to Michigan, and we all hope this move is really what she wants. She sold her mobile here and also her home in Florida. We had bought her 5<sup>th</sup> wheel last year. Jackie has family back in Michigan and we all feel that there are just too many memories here.

It has been 8 weeks since Mandy died and we still think of her daily and miss her so very much, but haven't reached the point of looking for another dog yet. Our friends Jack and Linda Kershles from Massachusetts will be here in July, so we are looking forward to their visit.

June 14th. We went halibut fishing yesterday and between 7 of us only 3 small fish were caught, but we did come back to camp and pigged out on fresh deep fried halibut. In a couple of weeks we will be going inland about 80 miles to fish on the Russian and Kenai rivers for sockeye salmon and then our smoking and canning kicks into high gear.

So far this has been a relaxing summer and the weather has improved greatly since we arrived in Homer, but here it is the 14th of June already and we will be heading home before we know it. The next three weeks I will work 4 days a week and then slack off for Jack and Linda's visit.

We went clamming across the bay and had a wonderful clam feast again. Now we will bag up and freeze the rest for the rest of the summer. Jerry has 2 more king salmon to smoke and then I will vacuum pack it. Jackie left today, bound for Michigan with all her belongings that she could fit in her pickup. We couldn't help feeling sad in knowing that she most likely will live to regret the move and the finality of it. It seemed like we lost Jackie as well as Bud and it all seemed so final.

Jun 21st, Fathers Day. We met Tom and Jean for breakfast at 9 am and then went on their boat halibut fishing. It was an absolutely beautiful day, waters were calm and we headed for their favorite spot. The limit is 2 halibut per person per day and the 4 of us limited out in 3 hours. Tom got a 100 pounder and the rest of us got 20 to 40 pound fish. We then headed across the bay to Halibut Cove (which I have mentioned before). We had our usually wonderful feast while sitting on the outside deck, basking in the sun. The dark beer was good too! But the highlight of my day was having the baby harbor seal come to me as I sat on the dock. He was swimming close to the dock and came and brushed his little mouth and whiskers on my hand. I was thrilled to say the least and it's been hard to think of anything else since that special, perhaps once in a lifetime experience. The baby seal was one of the seals that was being rehabilitated and cared for after the oil spill and was now back in the water and free to leave.

Jack and Linda called today and will arrive in Anchorage July 15th. We will meet them at the airport and then pick up their leased conversion van and proceed to show them the highlights of Alaska. Jack has been here before, but this is Linda's first trip.

TOM AND JEAN AT HALIBUT COVE

June 30th we went to the Moose Pig Roast in Kenai last Saturday, and a fun time was had by all. It was great to see familiar faces that we have met over the years. After the dinner we continued north approximately 50 miles to the Russian River (where everyone else was). We did manage to get into the parking area at the ferry and went to sleep. The next morning we got prepared for our long day of fishing. You have to pack everything to go across the river, food, extra clothing, fishing gear and cameras. The little ferry takes you across a 200 foot span to the other side, and once there you join the other combat fisherman in their attempts to catch the elusive sockeye.

We had quite a day (10 hours of fishing) to catch our limit of 3 fish per person. The fish are bigger this year with an average of 10 to 12 pounds and fighters they are for sure. The day ended with 6 fish for us and back across the river two tired souls went. The next day Jerry canned fish and I went to work.

On July 4th we attended the annual Elks Party and the highlight was a "golf scramble" set up on the beach! (While the tide was out), it sure was a lot of fun. The weather continues to be beautiful. The green foliage has taken over with beautiful blue lupine and crimson fireweed. I look out my window and I see the every day changing view of the mountains and the glaciers. There is still quite a lot of snow on the peaks and tonight the clouds are half way up the mountains, giving a spectacular view of the bay and the mountain peaks.

Jerry has been busy fixing this and that, just making the place look better every day.

July 11th and what a day (nearly our last), we left to go halibut fishing at 6 am. There was fog everywhere, but we went out any way. We left the harbor with Tom and Jean in their 24 foot boat and headed for our favorite spot. It takes about an hour to get to the area and we follow the steep cliffs and head north, to make the story short, we were moving along fairly fast when Jerry yelled "ROCK", well I want to say we didn't miss it by much and if we had struck it I doubt I'd be writing this. Hitting the rock would do us in and if it didn't, we were approximately ¾ of a mile off shore in 38 to 40 degree water. The rest of the day was rain, more fog and little fish! I caught a cod and Jean caught a 110 pound halibut. We were delighted in seeing a whale surface and spouting and also several otters.

This is truly a land of beauty, mystery and intrigue, but also danger. There were two bear attacks in Alaska this past week, with both resulting in death, which serves to remind us that the beauty and the danger go hand in hand

We met Jack and Linda at the Anchorage Airport and took them to get their rented conversion van and then we headed down the peninsula to introduce them to all the wonderful sights that the area has to show. We stayed at Morgan's Landing for 2 days and stood in the Kenai River for hours at a time, (mostly in the rain). I lost 5 sockeye, Jerry caught 1, Jack none (even though he tried to convince us he had), but the truth came out that someone gave him one, and the novice in the group caught the biggest sockeye we had ever seen! We had a great time and one night the Park Ranger came by and told us to keep our voices down; we had forgotten how late it was in view of it being light till 1 am. We then headed down to Homer the next day. Jack and Linda went out with Tom and Jean for a day of halibut fishing and we canned salmon for them while they were gone. They got back around 3:30 and we met them at the harbor, unloaded the fish (Linda also caught the biggest halibut too!) and then we went across the bay to share the beauty of Halibut Cove with them.

Enroute they were able to see volcanoes, whales, otters and puffins. We came back home and took a drive up to the mountain ridge and saw a moose and came back to camp for a clam feast. Today I am the pressure cooker watcher for the canning of the halibut. Jack, Linda and Jerry went down on the Spit to get water, fish a while and Linda is checking out all the tourist shops.

July 27th and we have been busy doing what we like to do the most, Sockeye fishing, day and night. We have spent a few miles each week going back and forth between Homer and the Kenai River. So far we have caught 32 fish and everyone a fighter, we've lost so much tackle this year and we have a ways to go yet. We've canned eleven cases and now we'll smoke the rest we get and can them too. I can't believe that we leave for home in 4 weeks. It has been raining on and off for over 3 weeks.

The fireweed is almost flowered out to the top; the days continue to get shorter and cooler with rain. September brings early snows and that signals us to head south. We spent the last two days acting like regular tourists. We took off and camped out, visited Seward which lies along the south central coast and is approximately 120 miles south of Anchorage by way of the Seward Highway (or can be reached by water). Seward is named for William H. Seward who was credited for arranging the Alaska purchase from Russia. We hiked to Exit Glacier, which is a close up experience to a beautiful blue glacier. We were able to hike right up to the base and it sure was a sight.

EXIT GLACIER

Seward is approximately 165 miles northeast of Homer and is a must of towns to visit. On the way back to Homer, we stopped at Quartz Creek and watched the sockeye at life's end. The fish turn all red and take on a grotesque shape and eventually die out.

August 10th and I have three more shifts at work. Today we go out in the big commercial boat to drop crab pots. A short period is open for subsistence only (this is for residents only and non-commercial).

August 14th and we pulled up the crab pots and if you've ever thought you'd died and went to heaven! That was our feeling exactly. They had gotten a lot of crab and we were very glad to be their guests. We ate and ate and ate some more!

August 19th and our time is drawing near! Yesterday we picked 2 ½ gallons of wild blueberries right in the woods behind our trailer and had fresh pie and I made 8 jars of jam and froze the rest. Last night Mt. Spur "blew its top" and rained volcanic ash all aver Anchorage and today we could smell sulfur like smell in the air. There are no flights in or out of Homer, as well as Anchorage due to the ash in the air.

August 24th and weather in the news again, only this time in Florida. Hurricane Andrew spared Pine Island, but still waiting for the water surge. The area of Homestead really got hit hard. Also we hear that Glacier National Park got two feet of snow and we go through that area when we leave our son's place in Montana.

Today it is dark, cloudy and pouring down rain. We will finish our closing of our trailer today and tomorrow we will leave for Soldotna, before heading on to Anchorage.

We looked back on our little Alaska Home, as we drove out the drive. We both look forward to going home, but also will miss Homer. It was a little easier to leave though in view of the very windy, cold and rain, rain and more rain. The mountains here have already gotten their first dusting of snow and the trees are all varied hews of yellow and they too have been dusted, only with volcanic ash and it looks like pale concrete dust.

August 28th we stayed in Tok last night and you could see your breath this morning. We decided to go the Taylor Highway once again in hopes of seeing the tens of thousand migrating caribou to their southern winter home of Valdez, Alaska. We have been winding around through the remnants of the old gold mines and then back up the mountains with the sharp switch backs. Most of the time we are above the clouds. Eventually we will be above the tree line with nothing but tundra. The history here is mind jolting as we come across what's left of an old cabin by a rushing stream and also the occasional remnants of old gold mines.

Here we sit at Laird Hot springs; we have a roaring bonfire and have already soaked in the hot springs. Jerry is preparing the steaks. It is warmer here and we will stay here at one of our favorite spots for several days. They have posted additional "Bear Danger Signs", so we will be on the watch. We meet so many people that do much like we do, and now they are on their way back to somewhere in the lower 48 too. So, our summer has come to an end, until Alaska "One More Time."

# OLE BLUE

April 30th, 1993 and we are departing again for our Alaska home, only this time we leave in real comfort. We purchased a 32 foot "Excalibur" motor home with all the creature comforts. Jerry had major surgery this past January and we felt it was time to travel a little more in style and comfort; we will sell the 5th wheel when we get to Homer.

WE HAVE GROWN

We drove to Valdosta, Georgia the first night and stayed in a beautiful rest area. We woke up to a beautiful morning with moss laden oak trees surrounding us. This traveling in such comfort can grow on you real quick. What a difference to be able to stand upright, that you couldn't do in the van.

We also have a new passenger on board and her name is Brandy, another poodle and she is the color of brandy, and a little bundle of energy. We got her last September and after being without "Mandy" for five months, felt it was time.

BRANDY

The dogwood trees are in full bloom and absolutely beautiful. We are going a little different route this year. We are headed for Maggie Valley, North Carolina to see a cousin of Jerry's, who owns a resort there. He has a 30 room motel and a restaurant. Last night the rooms were all filled with a motorcycle rally. The sound of "Harley's" filled the town. This area truly is a valley, the mountains shoot straight up behind the variety of buildings and homes dot the various elevations. We will spend the day here and leave for Michigan tomorrow.

On the road again, after visits in Michigan with our daughter and family also Jerry's sister and brother and their families, then on to northern Michigan to have time with my Mom and my brothers and sisters.

We woke to rain, but fairly warm yet. They must have had a tremendous amount of snow here, as the fields and streams are all water. Rivers are overflowing and we are now 37 miles east of Grand Rapids, Minnesota.

7 pm and we are now in the rolling hills of North Dakota. It continues to be warm and all you see are barren hills for miles and miles and in-between are freshly plowed fields. Spring has sprung!

Well!!! Another first, I took a shower while traveling down the road at 60 miles per hour, you do what you have to do when your driver wants to keep driving all night. It worked out great, not to far to fall in a little shower.

10:45 pm and just came through Glascow, Montana, roads are rough, area is still in rolling hills, no trees and government housing dots the landscape. This is Indian Territory. It's going to be in the 90s today and down to 40 tonight. Our critters of the day were 2 buffalo, horses and crows.

May 12th and at 2 pm we just got a glimpse of the Rocky Mountains with their snow covered peaks, seems so unlikely in view of it being 90 degrees.

We are now going through the south end of Glacier National Park and snow is even along sides of the road and it is still 80 degrees.

May 14th, we spent a short visit with our son, and family in Libby, Montana. The girls are growing up to fast. We are now in Jasper, Alberta getting a new fuel filter on, but let me back up a little. We had quite an eventful day yesterday, it started with leaving Libby at 7:30 am. We arrived at the Canadian border and received more than our usual hassle. I'm convinced we must look like drug dealers. They went through the entire coach, looking for hand guns, alcohol, cigarettes and/or drugs. We received a stern warning for carrying a loaded shotgun (in a case), which we thought was ok. Get this logic! They asked why we carry a gun and we told them it was for protection. They informed us we could transport it for protection from the bears but not people, and of course I had to tell them it wasn't the bears we were concerned about. Once again they gave us a lecture telling us they could take the gun and refuse us entry, but because we had been honest they were letting us through. That incident just started our day. It was still extremely warm all day, even through the ice fields of the parks in Jasper. Very little snow on the peaks now and water falls all over. We had several problems with the motor home climbing at elevations of 6700 feet strained her to the max. The transmission over heated and was slipping we must have gotten water in our last load of gas as the engine was cutting out when Jerry would accelerate the gas petal.

We hit a big bump and the spring rod over the bathtub came down (with all the clothes), the cupboard above the stove with the microwave in it started to loosen and the refrigerator stopped working.

So after a few repairs, everything is back to working, now we are at a lumber company getting some doweling supports for the cupboard. Coming through the parks was not the best idea with this big of a unit and we never gave it a moments thought. We saw our usual assortment of animals, only a lot fewer. Black bears, mountain sheep, elk, deer, prairie dogs (no grizzly), to warm I guess.

I had my driver's lesson back in Minnesota and it went well, so now according to my husband I'm a "qualified motor home driver", no backing up though! Jerry is doing a great job of driving and also fixing things as they break down.

4 pm, and east of Grand Prairie, Alberta. It continues to be warm, no snow. We are out of the mountains, until we reach Ft. Nelson. We got our first tank of gas in Canada, $120.00 for a fill up and we will have to fill 3 more times in Canada.

May 15th. We spent our night in Dawson Creek, mile 0 of the Alaskan Highway. We even watched TV for first time on this journey. Woke up to a sunny morning again, T-shirt weather, per Jerry. We need to stop at the "butcher block meat market" for steaks, garlic sausage and other supplies at this favorite market and then we will head for Ft. Nelson which is 300 miles away.

May 16th and we arrived at Laird River late last night and stayed outside the park till this morning. The trip continued to be a lot warmer than usual and little or no snow on the mountains in this area. We saw reindeer, deer, mountain sheep and one moose. Roads are very rough with the spring thaw. We came upon an area of thick smoke and off in the distance was a forest fire spreading up the mountains.

At the present time Jerry is shaving outside, we are in our swimsuits, temperature is about 80 degrees and we just came back from our soak in the hot springs. This year is so different from the previous trips with the foliage out in comparison to last year with the bushes bare and one was able to see the next camp site. We cooked breakfast outside (all fat free).

LAIRD HOT SPRINGS CAMP SITE

Update on forgotten events: So far we have left behind one remote unit for the motor home alarm system, I left it on a picnic table in North Carolina and the outdoor mat was left in Dawson Creek.

We picked mushrooms in Michigan and will have them on steaks tonight. The motor home has been running good with exception of the transmission slipping when doing a lot of climbing and the temperature is in the 80s and we will check in Anchorage about having a transmission cooler put on, other wise everything is ok. We have gotten as high as 9.3 miles per gallon and as low as 7.6 and usually averaging around 8.3 and were happy with that with a unit this big.

May 17th and we awoke to rain here at Laird Hot Springs and decided to break camp and head west, so much for spending a couple of days here, but we can't complain when yesterday we were able to set outside in our bathing suits. Its cooler today and the further northwest we head, the cooler it becomes. Snow is at the lower elevations now and some of the lakes are frozen over. We came through a lot of construction with gravel and mud. Lizzy needs a bath.

Tonight we are parked at the visitor center in Whitehorse. We called our friend; Hank Karr and met him for coffee. It is so nice to spend time with friends that we have met on previous trips and hopefully he will be able to visit us in Homer this summer. Hank is Canadian and his wife is American, they have lived in Whitehorse for 28 years and we met them through a friend in Florida. Shorty used to play in a band with Hank over 10 years ago in Alaska. This year we filmed Shorty while he was playing at the VFW in Ft. Myers and brought the film to Hank. Last year we filmed Hank in Whitehorse and took the film to Shorty.

We spent a terrible day on the road yesterday, 170 miles of extreme road conditions, mostly under construction. We spent the night at a Tok, Alaska campground. We appreciated all the creature comforts such as showers, laundry and a bath for Lizzy too. The weather turned warm, 65 degrees and snow still on the mountain tops. We treated ourselves to lunch out and now headed for Anchorage 325 miles away.

8:30 pm and we had a beautiful drive today, warm and the visibility of the mountain tops were breathtaking. We are now camped beside the Matanuska River which is 75 miles east of Anchorage. It is warm (65 to 70) and the soothing sounds of the fast current will provide for good sleeping. Brandy had her first day of "car sickness" and has been very quiet all day after of two episodes of upchucking, so she is enjoying the down time I'm sure.

May 24th and we are back in our second home of Homer, Alaska after spending 3 days in Anchorage stocking up with supplies for the summer. We spent our first day here getting organized with putting all the supplies away in the gear shed. Tonight we just came from our friends; Tom and Jean Schroeder and the wonderful supper that they fixed. It always makes us feel so at home to see old friends. Tomorrow I go to the hospital to check my schedule for the summer. The view out the window here is Kachemak Bay and the glaciers across the bay. The mountains still have lots of snow and the temperature is to go down to the 40's tonight.

May 24th and today was a busy one. I was up to the hospital to get my schedule and I go to work on the 28th on the 3 to 11 shift and so far through the June schedule I'll work 2 or 3 days a week which is great. I spent the rest of the day doing laundry and continued to try and organize and unload our 5th wheel to get it ready to sell. We have much duplication, and I will spend the next couple of days trying to sort it out and then on Thursday we go fishing for king salmon and can hardly wait.

No fishing today, to much work to do. We showed the 5$^{th}$ wheel trailer all day and think we have it sold already. Beautiful weekend forecast for the upcoming Memorial Day Holiday.

May 30$^{th}$ and the trailer is sold and gone and we got the asking price. Worked last night and so good to see familiar faces at work, some of which I have worked with since 1989. Yesterday we went fishing in the Cook Inlet with Tom and Jean and we all limited out on halibut, (2 each) and 4 cod. The weather has been beautiful and so clear that we were able to see the Barren Islands that are in the inlet north of Kodiak Island. It seems so strange to be able to see a distance of 80 to 100 miles. Last night we were sitting in the motor home and Mrs. Moose and her baby came to feed only 15 feet from the motor home.

Today I fixed halibut for everyone and tomorrow we go to Tom and Jean's annual Memorial Day picnic. As I'm writing this, I'm looking out the window and it is still light out at midnight. The mountains across the bay are sharply visible, including the peaks with no clouds and just clear blue skies. You can see the lights of the various oil tankers that are parked in Kachemak Bay awaiting clearance to head up the Cook Inlet. The village here is filled with campers to enjoy the fishing for king salmon. We will go fishing on Tuesday after all go back home from the holiday.

The memorial picnic was great and very warm and truly enjoyed by all. Tom and Jean sure put on a great feast for all and Cotton Moore does his usual tremendous job with his BBQ ribs and chicken.

The event of today is to try and describe the vehicle Jerry bought. It was decided to only spend enough for transportation for while we're here in Homer, and that's probably good because this "piece of transportation" would be risky at going more than 10 miles away. He bought a 1974 "cherry" Chevelle, color blue and rust!!! With bald tires and air conditioned (natural.....holes in the floorboard), but so far runs good and I'll keep all updated.

Today is a semi-relaxing day, clean coach, change beds, make bread and have friends for dinner. I'm on call today and need to stick close to home. I picked rhubarb and made a cobbler. Last night Mrs. Moose came by with the twins and stopped right by the motor home and nursed her babies. It has turned somewhat cooler and windy. Jerry is having a ball working on his "blue machine". This car looks so bad, he surely will be stopped by the police and thought to be one of the transient druggies, but any way he is having fun with it. I just hope he doesn't want to restore it.

We have been very busy, our friends Fred and Barbara Moehle from Massachusetts arrived and Fred and Barb were very good sports about riding in "OLE BLUE."

OLE BLUE BEFORE THE PAINT JOB

AFTER THE PAINT JOB

Just before Fred and Barb arrived, I got my first king salmon and 1 hour later got my second one. They both were about 20 to 25 pounds each and what a thrill to catch as they give such a fight. I truly am hooked on salmon fishing. Friday night we had fresh halibut and cod fish. Saturday we were fishing for kings at 4:30 am, breakfast at 8 am and picking mussels by 9:30 am. We pigged out on our earlier work at night.

Sunday, up at 6 am and went north about 40 miles to go razor clamming at Clam Gulch and had another feast......sooooo good. Fred wasn't convinced that razor clamming was worth all the work.

Today was Barb's turn to show all how to catch king salmon, two within a very short time and was going for the third when gently informed by fish and game officer that two was the limit per day. The guys were a little bent out of shape when out done by the girls and Fred said he would hear about the catch all the way back to Massachusetts.

Tomorrow back to work, we have already canned two cases of kings, smoked and cleaned mussels and got four containers in the freezer. Jerry and Tom went fishing for halibut and came back with their limit, so into the freezer went several meals of halibut.

BARB AND HER KINGS

Hospital census is down, so I haven't worked much and I'm enjoying the free time. Tomorrow we get ready for Thursday's trip to Anchorage and a friends wedding (no we won't be taking Ole Blue) we will take the motor home. Ole Blue is still running (much to my surprise) and Jerry pampers it like it was worth a cool million.

June 22$^{nd}$ and catch up time again. The wedding was very nice and we also found time to stock up on supplies. Now we are back in Homer and Jerry is smoking fish. Weather continues to be very sunny and warm and do hope it lasts.

It's getting close to the time that we head up north about 90 miles to fish on the Russian and Kenai River for the red salmon. This is perhaps our favorite type of fishing, the river is very fast and when you connect with the fish they fight to the end.

June 30th and catch up time again. We almost got skunked on the Russian River; Jerry got one and lost four. I lost one and that was it; the early run was over and we missed it. We left the Russian River and headed south, stopping at Morgan State Park and checking on the progress of the revamping of our favorite park. Before the revamping one could park anyplace with no designated space and it was more fun and more campers were accommodated. With the new park, there will be approximately 50 sites and it will keep the amount of people down at any given time on the river, which is the overall goal. Fish and Game officials are concerned about the river banks being eroded and have put up barriers to limit the public to those banks. There are now designated areas with boardwalks to fish from.

We left Morgan's and continued on to Soldotna and to Funny River Campground on the south side of the Kenai River. We looked up friends that we had met several years earlier (Spencer's) from Texas. They are the hosts at this campground this year and this is where we sit now at our campsite in the woods with a field of wild flowers of every color and a well trampled moose trail. It was so fun to watch Brandy as she attacked a low lying bush with so much aggression that we wondered what she thought it was.

We went to the annual 4th of July party at the Elks Club in Homer. An employee of the hospital won the grand prize of $12,500. We fished for halibut on the 5th; I got a 40 pound (Jerry got skunked this time). I spent most of the next day vacuum packing it. Today we canned 2 cases of sockeye.

We spent the last few days with Lee and Dee Jones, from Muskegon, Michigan. They are friends of our friend Donna and she suggested they look us up. They will take their 5th wheel up to the Kenai River next week with us to try and get our fill of sockeye.

July 11th, would you believe…81 degree's? People here say this is a first in 30 years.

Here we sit on a bank overlooking the Kenai River. The area here at Morgan's is a mess. They didn't get the campground opened yet and they have a lot of *#*!X* off people and almost including us, but after a lot of "gentle persuasion" (begging) we finally got a place to park. Lee and Dee Jones are next to us.

Fishing was great and we caught our limit of 3 per person in 3 hours. The weather continues to be unbelievable and every day we get up to sun.

RED, LEE AND DEE AND THEIR SALMON

THE WORK BEGINS

RED AND ROSE, TWO TIRED FISHERMEN

Tonight we watched the fishing fleet come in to the harbor in Soldotna. It is a sight that you will never forget. The fleet of boats is returning with their catch and heading for cannery. The weather continues to be very warm and we are having a great time with our new friends, thanks to Donna for arranging us to meet.

July 21st, and we are back in Homer. We caught our limit every day and now the work of canning begins. I have been continuing to work 2 to 3 days when I'm in town and the census is really up with all the tourists in town.

We have friends from California that will be coming August 5th. (Art and Fannie Mackie). Fannie and I worked together at a hospital in Punta Gorda, Florida in the 80s and have kept in touch since. They are based out of San Diego, California. Art is a pilot and Fannie is a flight nurse and they just set up air ambulance service in Juneau, Alaska. They transfer patients all over the world. So they will be here for 6 days and it will be fun to show them around, after that we will start to get ready to leave. We plan on leaving here August 14th and will take our time on the trip back home.

July 25th and we are back at Morgan's Landing and campground full, but we were put in overflow. The new park opened a few days ago. At 9 am we got a site and try and picture this, our view is to the north east, we are high above the river and the Kenai Mountains are in the distance with the view intermingled with the vast spruce trees and if that wasn't enough of natural beauty to please anyone there are vast amount of wild flowers. The fireweed really dominates with the bright magenta color. The fireweed flower is creeping to the top to signify the ending of summer soon. We continue to have great weather, today just a little cooler.

CAMP SITE AT MORGAN'S LANDING

Fish are not running real strong, so we are enjoying the rest and will try later today.

August 7th. Our stay at Morgan's was great and again we limited out once the fish started running. We came home and smoked and canned. Now we are done and have 12 cases and fish in the freezer. Our time is growing short and we leave in 13 days. Our friends Fannie and Art arrived yesterday. They flew from Juneau to Anchorage and rented a motor home. This morning we are going fishing on the Anchor River for silver salmon. Tonight we have planned a clam bake and tomorrow we're sending them out with Tom and Jean for a day of halibut fishing and then later in the day a trip with the six of us to Halibut Cove. We fished at the fishing hole (or rather we snagged) as snagging was open for a few days for pink salmon and Fannie had a ball and snagged 8 pinks, Art got 4 and I got 2 pinks and 1 big silver (none for Jerry), he spent his time taking care of our fish.

FANNIE AND ART

FANNIE SNAGGING THE PINKS

ART GOT ONE TOO

Today we got up early and meet Tom and Jean for breakfast and then saw the four of them off for a day of halibut fishing. We came back to camp to can the fish caught yesterday for Fannie and Art to take home. It was a beautiful day in the 70's and we are waiting for them to radio in to us to meet at the boat harbor.

Oh yes! Jerry sold "OLE BLUE" to a teenage boy who thinks it is a corvette in disguise and he picks up the car on the 17th and I do believe we will miss the ole girl, we've had a lot of fun with our Homer car. Jerry decided she needed TLC to make it through the winter, so sacrificed her to a teenager.

Yes!! Fannie got her halibut, all 80 pounds and she is still on cloud nine to say the least. She even gave her fish a name, "George" and we are not going to hear the last of this fish story for some time to come. Today it is misting and overcast, but warm. We have 9 more days here. Summer for us has passed quickly; I'm working the next 3 days and then 1 day off and then work the 15th for the last shift of this year.

ART, TOM, "GEORGE", FANNIE AND JEAN

August 20th. Today we leave and with mixed feelings, as this is also home to us. It's always hard to leave friends and co-workers and Homer itself. Today it may be a little easier in view of the weather being rainy, foggy and cold, so up the road we go.

The mountains have received their first dusting of snow. We stopped at "Porcupine State Park", parked by a stream and cooked southern fried chicken, mashed potatoes, dressing and biscuits. It was time for a break from our fish diet. We ran into miles of bad roads, fog and rain. The leaves have already turned yellow and orange and falling off the trees.

Aug 23rd. We are at Dawson City and what a day we've had. We traveled the "Top of the World Highway" which starts north about 12 miles east of Tok, Alaska. This is the third time we have come this route and for sure the last!!!. It was 187 miles of nightmare. Snow, fog, slippery conditions on sheer cliffs and when it wasn't snowing, it was raining. Most of the driving is above the tree line and once you reach the Canadian border you are only about 85 miles from the Artic Circle. We came this way because Jerry saw a hat here last year and decided he had to have it. He may wear it or eat it….if he even finds it. We made it to Dawson City and Jerry is washing the mud off the motor home. Tomorrow he will get the hat (hopefully). Note….the hat is probably made in China.

We are now heading to Whitehorse from Dawson City, some 335 miles of mostly paved road. Weather is still cold, rain with forecast of snow. Jerry did find his hat (made in Canada) it looks good on him and he even tipped it at me….gee, maybe it will make a country gentleman out of him. Brandy continues to be a good traveler with the exception of bridges with overhead structures; she really panics and becomes very fearful, so now we hide her face before going through one.

August 26th. It was the coldest yet…26 degrees and the furnace ran most of the night. We are heading for Laird River with a stop in Watson Lake for some supplies. We bought steak for $16.98 per pound (ouch).

Arrived at Laird River and what a difference in the temperature, it is warm and sunny. We went for a hot soak and now a nice bonfire. Brandy is being teased by the abundant amount of squirrels.

Still at Laird and soaking in the springs three times a day. Had a bear visit our camp site last night, but we never saw the outside of him, but he left a big pile of his insides 15 feet from the motor home and the park ranger nicely cleaned it up. Oh yes; we had the steaks and they were delicious and have to retract the cost. I read the print with glasses and discovered it said $16.98 per kg not pound. It made us feel a lot better.

August 30th. We are heading for Prince George, BC and then on to the state of Washington. I thought I would include this part of the journey home, because it took us to some very interesting places. We camped in a beautiful provincial park approximately 400 miles south of Prince George. The trees were huge ponderosa pine. We built a fire and sat watching it for hours in pitch black darkness (in bear country). Tomorrow we will be back in USA and decent gas prices we hope. We have driven over 1800 miles through Canada at prices averaging $2.80 per gallon.

The temperature has gotten really warm. It got up to 73 degrees today. We put in a weather station, which gives us inside and outside temps.

We are winding our way through the mountains in a canyon with a beautiful river along side. We are on US 97 south in Washington, approximately 150 miles north of Yakima, Washington. This area is not what we pictured. It is barren mountains and apple orchards. We are filling our appetites with fresh fruit. Last night was another new experience, we checked out the state park and decided the supermarket parking lot looked a lot cleaner (and free) and so did 23 other travelers in RV's, mostly from British Columbia. Everyone seemed to do a lot of shopping; maybe it was because it was cheaper in the US.

We spent last night in a campground on the banks of the Columbia River in The Dalles, Oregon. We descended into a steep canyon before reaching the river and stayed at this unique park. Every camp site had its own peach tree and peaches were free for the picking. We picked mostly from the ground and left with quite a lot. We left the park and headed south on US 97. Our lunch sight was at 4800 feet on top of a mountain ridge, with Mt. Hood for our landscape.

On to the north side of Crater Lake National Park, and I want to tell you it is one beautiful sight and to think that this was created from a volcanic explosion and it looks just like its name, "Crater Lake". The lake has the bluest of water and is approximately 9 miles wide. Like I said, it was beautiful, but I never want to travel north to south on it again. First of all the road isn't made for large motor homes and I was on the cliff side. There are no guard rails and you are between 12 to 14 inches from kissing your butt good bye and when you are sitting up high it seems worse. The cliffs are straight down for hundreds of feet and my knees were getting weak. We make it to the south side and camped by a deep ravine in a park where bears are numerous. We canned 12 jars of jam out of our peaches and a delicious supper before turning in.

September 4th. We came through Reno, Nevada yesterday and when I say came through....what a concrete jungle, I guess we've been in Alaska to long because we are beginning to avoid crowds and traffic. We continued on through and resisted the urge to stop and visit the casinos. We found a campground; NOW!!! This campground was in a mountain side and a level site was not to be found, but with a little help of boards under the tires we managed.

Another beautiful day and another experience. We got up early and headed for Lake Tahoe. Jerry decided to put the motor home to the test....new transmission now or later. We climbed to 8600 feet. The lake was breathtaking and surely a rich man's paradise. We descended down a 9% grade for 7 miles. The brakes started smelling and I thought...oh boy, it's forever land for us, but we made it and didn't learn our lesson. We decided to go from east to west through Yosemite National Park. We had been there before, but had not gone clear through and came in from the west.

We entered the park by climbing to 9941 feet and the motor home ran fine. The scenery was breathtaking beauty with shear cliffs again and my legs turned to jelly. We came upon a mountain lake and stopped to talk with people that were fishing for lake trout and before you knew it .....Jerry was "Indian Trading" smoked salmon for fresh lake trout. Now we have 2 lake trout and the Japanese guys were extremely happy with the smoked fish.

We continued on, winding in and around the shear cliffs. I'm not kidding when I say you are on the "edge of death" constantly, as you wind around the turns and approximately 9000 feet high. The campgrounds in the park were all full as we expected they would be on a Labor Day holiday. We headed for the big grove of sequoia trees and got there only to discover that we couldn't take our motor home up the 2 miles to the grove. The sign said anything over 26 feet had to park and could take the free shuttle; except the shuttle closed at 6 pm and now it was 6:30. So......no place to stay and we continued on for 20 more miles and now we are in a parking lot of a medical plaza. We set up our gas grill and did steaks and so ended our holiday.

We drove up to the sequoias the next day and when you see the huge trees, you can hardly believe what your looking at and certainly a must see sight on this trip.

September 6th, and the view out our window is the Mojave Desert. The coffee tastes great after a good rest last night. This part of the world is barren with exception of cactus, sagebrush and treeless mountains. We drove from Yosemite till late last night to make it across this unbearable heat. It was 98 degrees on our temperature gauge. Tonight we are in Laughlin, Nevada (Disney World for adults). This is a casino town and we are at the Riverside Resort campground, which is right on the casino strip. It is 109 degrees at 8 pm. We gambled until 2 am, ate breakfast and went to bed.

September 8th, at 10:30 in the morning and it is 103 degrees, but we are comfortable with our air conditioning. Yesterday was fun, no big win, but no big loss either. Two days of playing and eating and we are still ahead $30.00.

Guess this about ends our trip of 1993; we will be home in a few days and already planning for our next trip to "Alaska One More Time."

# WAGON MASTER

May 4th, 1994 and we are embarking on yet another trip to Alaska. This trip will be a very different one for us and very special as we will be leading a caravan of friends to experience the beauty of the trip. Our "Wagon Master" will be my husband Jerry, (Red) and he is looking forward to sharing all of his knowledge of making the trip over the years.

We once again leave from our home in Florida in our Excalibur motor home and head north on Interstate 75. We spent our first night in Tennessee, 125 miles south of Knoxville. We stayed in a rest area. Used our converter and watched TV. A van pulling a horse trailer parked beside us and took the horse out for a ride, got back in and left the horse evidence behind. We moved a little further down the street and turned in for the night.

We arrived in Grand Rapids, Michigan and parked at our daughter Carla's and husband Stan's home. Jerry had to fix the toilet (water leak), but otherwise everything running smooth. We awoke to snow the next morning and headed further north (should be south).

We visited with family and friends in northern Michigan and met with the three couples who would be making the adventure. We all met at my mother's house in Charlevoix, Michigan. Lee and Dee Jones from Muskegon, Michigan arrived first. We had spent time with them last year, fishing on the Kenai. John and Donna Martin from Pine Island, Florida arrived shortly after.

May 13th and the wagon train heads west. We awoke to 27 degree weather. Allen and Shirley Steckling from St. Helen, Michigan (and also winter residents of Pine Island, Florida arrived this morning.) The Wagon Master started us out at 9 am and we all said good bye to my mother and sister and left following our leader.

We crossed the Mackinaw Bridge and then headed west on US 2. Stopping for lunch outside in 42 degree weather was certainly different (especially those of us coming from Florida). By 4:30 it was 70 degrees and we stayed at the rest area on the Michigan/Wisconsin border. The trees are still bare here and evidence of dirty piles of snow can be seen. We stopped at the American Legion Post, and had a delicious fish fry in a very friendly post. The next morning we continued on in a very

157

hard rain and fog. We took an unscheduled tour of Duluth, Minnesota compliments of the Wagon Master (he took a wrong turn) and tried to convince all that he was just showing them the city....oh well.

May 15th we are quite a sight as we all caravan west. Three motor homes and one 5th wheel and truck. We stopped at a picnic area for a surprise birthday potluck for Dee and a very special cake, a 2 layer homemade by Donna. It consisted of 1 square layer and 1 round one. Out here you work with what you have. After the potluck we continued on to a truck stop and nestled in for the night.

We woke up to 34 degrees, but sunny. Today we head for Montana and the Wagon Master is going to let me have a real shower (he is loading up with water).

May 16th and picture this! We are sitting at a road side rest area in this town of Chester, Montana (a Lion's Club Rest Area), still on US 2 and all the guys are in deep trouble!! They went to the local Vets Club down and across the street and proceeded to get totally wiped out, especially the Wagon Master and Lee.

After two days of rest (some had hangovers), we headed out again for the west. The rest did me good. I'll back up a little, on May 7th I developed a pain in my left chest and it didn't go away so we stopped into a hospital in Traverse City, Michigan. I got the works, EKG, monitor, chest x-ray and lab work. The doctor said he thought I might be developing pneumonia and if I started having chills, fever and cough to start on the antibiotic prescription. Well...guess what 2 days later, chills, fever and cough and down right sick. I am feeling much better now.

May 19th and we are on Highway 93 south of Banff National Park in Alberta, Canada We spent last night at a KOA park in West Glacier, Montana. It rained all night. We just stopped for lunch. We do really well with the trip. The Wagon Master gives us daily schedules and we follow. Our destination today is the train station in Jasper, Alberta. There is a city park there and we have parked there year after year. The trains run and switch all night so one doesn't get much sleep (but it's free).

A STOP FOR LUNCH   ~   DEE, BRANDY AND ROSE

It took us 12 hours of traveling through the national parks to reach Jasper. It rained most of the day and cold, such a contrast to last years 90 degrees. We saw 4 black bears, deer, coyote, geese and several herds of elk.

May 21st. Our day turned out not to good, yesterday the left front tire on John's motor home was wearing and pulling, making it hard to steer. We stopped at Valley View, British Columbia at a garage and they told him they could fix it so we sent the others on to Dawson Creek and we stayed with John and Donna. Well it turned out they couldn't fix it, so we then limped on in to Grand Prarie and managed to get it fixed just before they closed for a 4 day Canada Holiday (the Queen's birthday). That was only the beginning of a bad day that only got worse. Donna twisted her ankle while getting out of the motor home and it was swelling with a lot of pain. We stopped at the ER in Dawson Creek and the x-rays revealed a hairline fracture. The doctor gave her the choice of a cast for comfort measures or a walking boot and stay off of it for several days with a prognosis of at least 3 weeks of discomfort. She chose the boot.

May 22nd and we are camped on the shore of Muncho Lake in B.C. We had a very tasty potluck and finished the evening enjoying the view of the beautiful green waters of the lake with mountains for a background. Last night we camped by a river and were able to have our first campfire with hotdogs and all the trimmings. We had Donna out in the lawn chair and she was the only one who had to suffer the smoke, while all the rest of us could easily move away. Tomorrow we head for Laird River Hot Springs and if weather is nice, we will stay for 2 days before heading for the Yukon. We saw several caribou, moose and bighorn sheep today.

May 25th. We had two beautiful days at Laird River Hot Springs.

SEE NO EVIL, HEAR NO EVIL AND SPEAK NO EVIL
LEE, ALLEN, JOHN AND RED AT LAIRD HOT SPRINGS

Today it is raining again, we drove on Whitehorse, stocked up on needed supplies and drove on west of the city to a turnout area by a river. We also met another couple there who was headed for their summer home in Seward, Alaska. We all enjoyed happy hour outside with shrimp, crackers, cheese and other things to nibble on.

We woke up to a very cold morning…27 degrees. Ahead of us are the most terrible roads on the entire trip. We stopped for lunch, each in the comfort of their vehicle, then continued on and so far the roads have exceeded their reputation…..awful!!!!!. All of our rigs are covered with mud. The guys are feeling generous today and promised to take us out for dinner when we reach Tok, Alaska.

Finally we arrived in Tok. We were all very tired, everyone got a campsite and hooked up except us, we transported all, plus the couple we had met earlier to the restaurant a mile down the street "Fast Eddy's" a great place to eat.

The next day we woke to guess what? Yup...More rain and 34 degrees. We should have been happy with the rain as it soon turned to snow and I mean lots of snow, we are on our way to Anchorage and some of the highest elevation and switchbacks are on this leg of our journey. 8 inches had fallen here 2 nights ago and now we are in a full blown snow storm. Shirley was not to happy, most of all she doesn't like heights and especially on snow covered roads. We are still at lower elevations and wonder what lies ahead and no one has "snow chains". Remember we're from Florida!!!!!

We made it to Anchorage after hours of slow moving vehicles winding their way up and around the switch backs. All of the travelers had their nerves tested to the limit. We camped in "SAMS" parking lot.

May 28th. We are heading to Homer today. It is still overcast and difficult to see the big mountain range to our west. We are stocked with supplies for the summer. We all stopped at the "Bird House", a former "Chicken Coop", turned into a bar, one of the "must stops" in Alaska. The 1964 earthquake caused quite a shift in the floors, so the bar slopes too! And you really have to hang on to your drink. The interior has been decorated by various travelers, bras, pants, money and other assorted memorabilia.

DEE, ROSE AND JOHN IN THE 'BIRDHOUSE'

We arrived at the top of the hill overlooking Homer Harbor, what a sight,

HOMER SPIT

and it seems like we had just left here.

Now we are all working hard to sit up our camp sites. We toasted are arrival with Lee's homemade wine. And as if it was a prescheduled event" mamma moose came into camp to show off her twin calves, everyone was thrilled. Our sites overlook Kachemak Bay with the Kenai Mountain Range dotted with glaciers in the background. We are on the same property that we have stayed on over the years.

MAMMA MOOSE AND HER BABIES

May 29th, slept in till 10:30, we were really tired. We spent all day getting organized, had bean and ham soup, cornbread, homemade bread and salad for dinner, made by all. Tomorrow we attend the annual Memorial Day Picnic at Tom and Jean's house.

GETTING CAMP SET UP

The picnic was enjoyed by all and so good to see old and new friends. The weather even cooperated, 55 to 60 degrees (a regular heat wave). We all came back to camp with full bellies of chicken and ribs.....sooooo good. Tomorrow we get fishing licenses and get serious about this fishing.

ALLEN AND RED ENJOYING THE BBQ

DONNA, LEE AND ROSE SAVORING COTTON MOORE'S BBQ

June 3<sup>rd,</sup> my first day back at work and things are about the same. They are using the computer discharge instructions from the ER and that's nice. Came home about 3:30 and went fishing and caught my first 2 kings of the season. Jerry caught 1 yesterday and he also got 2 today. Al and John got theirs too. So tomorrow we smoke and can, while others of our group will be out trying their hand at halibut fishing.

ALLEN HARD AT WORK FISHING FOR KINGS IN THE FISHING HOLE

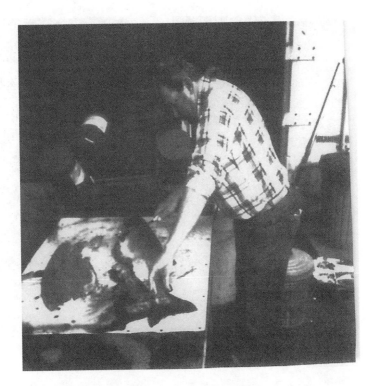

JOHN CLEANING HIS KING SALMON

DONNA, JOHN, ALLEN AND SHIRLEY

    June 7<sup>th</sup> and catch up time again. Our group has been to Halibut Cove across the bay. We've done some halibut fishing too! I caught 3; Jerry got 2, so we've been busy canning, smoking and also cutting brush and wood on the property here. We are all having a great time. Each day mother moose comes by to show the progress of her twin calves.

RED AND TOM WITH OUR HALIBUT CATCH

JOHN AND DONNA AT HALIBUT COVE

June 11th, we all have been busy, busy; fishing and more fishing, which means more work with canning and smoking. Jerry has already caught his limit of kings for the season (five is the total). I got another one which makes 3 for me. We went clamming the other day across the bay and dug for clams to our hearts content, came home, and all overate clams and mussels. The beach that we go to is across and up the bay 15 to 20 miles and only reached by boat or sea plane. The whole beach was covered with the large blue/black mussels.

DONNA AND SHIRLEY IN THE BOAT CABIN

Our group cook outs are extremely tasty, but bad for the waistline. Tomorrow we leave for the Russian River, 100 miles north for the first run of sockeye salmon.

Picture this! All four of our RV's lined up at 4 am to get into Morgan's State Park, you have to get there early in hopes of getting a site. I was making homemade doughnuts at this unheard of hour to keep all of our traveler's happy.

Last night we all met at our site and sampled multiple glasses of margaritas. A great time was had sitting around the camp fire and the group presented Jerry with a set of firewood tongs as a token for his "wagon master" skills.

June 16th and Al and Shirley left for home this morning, they had planned on only being gone 5 or 6 weeks. John, Donna, Dee and Lee and us are camped at Morgan's Landing State Park by Sterling, Alaska, and will go to the Russian River another 40 miles north tomorrow. Fish are in but slow. It seems like everything is late this year. Weather here is great and we've enjoyed the camp fires.

Tonight we've invited Don and Connie (the park hosts here), to a blackened halibut feast. They have been park hosts here for several years and are from Texas.

I sure have been lazy in writing: It is already June 24th. Our first trip to the Russian River came up with only 3 fish. Now we are here again and the fish are really running. The shoulder to shoulder "combat" fishing is well represented by various nationalities. Jerry and I caught our limit of 3 fish per person per day and it took us 8 hours to limit out. The limit changes with the amount of escapement up the river from the ocean. We had a thrill coming down here two days ago. Jerry picked me up from work at midnight. It was a full moon and about 2 am we came around a curve and Jerry glanced off to the right and there was an 8 to 10 foot tall grizzly standing looking at us. I guess the motor home looked big to him, because he dropped to all four and took off on a run. (I was glad we were in the motor home).

Once again I seem to be working more than planned, but once July 14th gets here, we will be at Morgan's Landing for about two weeks. On August 6th, John and Donna and us will leave for Denali National Park and then on to Fairbanks. This summer has gone by very fast; we are so busy all the time.

Busy night at work. Jerry is busy smoking all of our sockeye today. Weather has been great, sunny almost every day. John, Donna, Lee and Dee ventured off to Exit Glacier in Seward for a few days and should be back tomorrow. I forgot to mention that we bought "Ole Blue" back for the summer and the end of July we will once again sell it back to the same young guy who bought it last year. We are now looking forward to the annual July 4th picnic at the Elks Club and then on to fishing at Morgan's around the 14th of July.

Today John, Donna, Jerry and I took a ride to the top of Diamond Ridge in "Ole Blue". Now you have to imagine this!!! Ole Blue is held together by a lot of rust. Our great guys had put a bag of fish guts in the trunk, with intentions of taking it to the dump, (and forgot they put it there) Donna and I were riding in the back and the smell was unforgettable! Especially in view of the large hole between the trunk and the back seat, and if the smell didn't do you in the dust rolling in from the dirt roads did. Donna gave up using hair spray long ago.

July 26th, our lives have been turned upside down. On July 21st, our little dog; Brandy went to jump on the bed in the motor home and didn't quite make the complete leap. She hit her chest area on the edge of the bed and with difficulty pulled herself up the rest of the way. She whimpered during the night, but I thought she had just pulled her chest muscles. The next morning she just laid around, and not her usual playful self. John, Donna, Jerry and I left to go down to the river to fish (we were at Morgan's Landing). Jerry and John came back after several hours and Donna and I kept fishing for a while longer. When I arrived back to the camp site, I found Brandy dragging her hind legs. We rushed her to a vet in Soldotna, Alaska and his report to us was like hitting us in the heart. Brandy had a collapse of her thoracic vertebrae at the level of T12 and T13, and if that wasn't enough, he also told us she has an enlarged heart. He further suggested we have her operated on as soon as possible.

BRANDY

We found out that there was no vet in Alaska capable of doing the neurological procedure that Brandy required. The vet suggested that we fly her out to either Seattle or back to Florida. He gave her an injection of steroid and started her on one baby aspirin a day. We said a sad goodbye to all of our friends and headed back to Homer to gather belongings and to head home with our baby. (She is our baby). It was not an option to fly her out, as I wouldn't leave Jerry to drive out all alone. Jerry installed a hook at the very back of the coach (the bed is across the back), and when we were out of the coach we would hook Brandy to it and she would be safe on the bed. She had to be held all the time with only minimal walking allowed. After a few days she regained the use of her legs with the swelling down around her spinal cord. We are headed for the University of Florida in Gainesville, Florida with hopes of their being able to help her. Brandy is like our child and this is particular hard on us in view of this being the second time we have had to bring out a sick dog. Our Mandy had congestive heart failure in Alaska, treated in Whitehorse and nearly died on the trip home. She died 8 months later.

August 21$^{st}$, update…It took us 5 weeks to get home, roads were very rough. We had Brandy evaluated at Gainesville and we will take her back August 29$^{th}$ for surgery on her back. They wouldn't operate on her till she was off the aspirin for 10 days.

Brandy did very well with the surgery, if you can picture this little 11 pound dog with a 10 inch incision. The vets at University of Florida are the best and they treated her like a baby. We brought her home after 5 days and every thing went well for another week. We were not out of the woods yet. She started vomiting and after the second opinion and consulting back and forth with Gainesville, the diagnosis was acute kidney failure so back in the hospital again. We brought her home after a few days. She lost the tip of her tongue from the uremia. We had to force water down her every two hours to keep her kidneys flushed and after another month she was back to normal.

I am writing this chapter of the book on January 20, 2004 and Brandy is eleven and one half years old. She acts like a puppy and we treasure our years with her and hope to do "Alaska One More Time" with our little mascot.

# CABIN RETIREMENT

Our lives have changed a lot in the last three years since making our last trip to Alaska in 1994.

In May of 1996 we closed up our home in Florida and headed for our summer project of starting to build a cabin on our property in the north Georgia Mountains. We had purchased the property the previous year after realizing that we did not want to spend our retirement years in Florida. We are originally from Michigan and really began to miss the four seasons, and I'm sure our many trips to Alaska assisted in our decision. The north Georgia Mountains are very beautiful and our property is high and with long range views. We are surrounded by national forests and beautiful lakes and rivers. The project started by preparing a sight for the motor home, as that would be our summer home. I only stayed a few days, as I had to return to my job in Florida. Jerry returned to Florida the end of May and the plan was for me to take a four month summer leave and return to Georgia to continue the project. We received an unexpected call from a realtor that had showed our Florida property last February. We didn't even have the property listed now and he called and said the people that looked at it wanted to buy now. So our summer plans tuned out to be a permanent move to Georgia. We sold at the price we asked and the new owners paid cash and we never met them. (Some things are meant to be).

We worked all summer, fall and winter and finally moved into the cabin the first of April 1997 and the 15th of April closed the cabin and headed to Alaska "One More Time".

OUR CABIN

April 15th. We left home at 3 pm yesterday, drove to the Kentucky line on Interstate 75 and woke up to a blanket of frost at a Welcome Center, but we were snug and warm under several quilts that we brought for Alaska and needed them in Kentucky. It is bright and sunny and our view this morning is of rolling pasture land, lined with oak trees with dogwood intermingled.

It was somewhat difficult to leave our new cabin, part of us wanted to go and yet there was a tug to stay. If we get homesick, we can always come home early. The every day work on the cabin was getting to be a drain and coming home in the fall will be something to look forward to, especially with the major work done. Brandy is under her blanket and wants to head south instead of north.

April 16th and we've just come into the Michigan line and stopped at a rest stop. Our view is of trees (no buds), too cold, and it's like going back in time. We have come through areas of beautiful flowers, trees fully budded and then bare trees and no flowers. It is raining and very cool and the coffee tastes extra good this morning. We will be getting to Grand Rapids in a couple of hours to our daughter Carla and her husband Stan's home. We will spend the night and leave for Northern Michigan tomorrow. Carla will come up to Charlevoix, Michigan on Friday to help get ready for my mother's 80th birthday party on Saturday.

When we left Carla's there was snow on the ground, with a temperature of 22. We spent the night at Traverse City, Michigan at the VFW Lodge, a very friendly lodge. They offered us electric and the waitress even gave us all her bingo chips and daubers and we joined in for a night of bingo. We left in the morning for Sam's Club to meet my two sisters, Bea and Judy, to shop for the party.

April 20th and the party was great and mother really enjoyed her family and many friends who came to honor her. We left Charlevoix about 1pm and headed north. All the lakes are iced over, including Lake Michigan, piles of snow all over too. We parked for the night in a shopping plaza in Iron River, Michigan (about 80 miles east of the Wisconsin line). It is cool and we are just relaxing.

Just came into the Wisconsin line and now stopping at a rest area and having breakfast. We sure have seen a lot of deer. Also there is still a lot of snow to melt and the streams are already overflowing. We wonder what lies ahead of us as we go through Grand Forks, North Dakota and the floods there. Yesterday it was reported that 50,000 people were evacuated from the Red River Flood. We felt ok due to a misconception on our part that the river flows north to south and instead it flows south to north.

We are stopped for the night at Fisher, Minnesota and have had quite the experience. We traveled within sight of the flooded city of East Grand Forks, Minnesota. We could see just the top of the bridge that connects the two cities of East Grand Forks, Minnesota and Grand Forks, North Dakota. The rest of the bridge was under water. We were stopped at that point by police and were turned back. Why they didn't have a road block sooner is beyond us. The police stated the entire town of 50,000 people, have been evacuated and the entire city is under 30 feet of water.

We had started to see entire fields turned into lakes about 10 miles before we reached the city and we knew there was a flood, but not of this magnitude. We turned back and went about 7 to 10 miles and stopped at a rest area. We are so tired and decided to stay here for the night, there is still water everywhere, but we are at least 5 feet above the high water and hope the motor home doesn't turn into a boat.

The following morning we watched truck after truck of the National Guard go by. We headed back east to Crookston, Minnesota and then with the intent to go south to Fargo, N. Dakota and then back to heading west.

12:45 pm and we just stopped and made lunch, you would not believe how our day has gone so far. We left the rest area at 7:30 am and headed back to Crookston, stopped for gas and was told Highway 9 was open all the way south to US 10. We found 9 and started down it, water everywhere, houses submerged and we got about 7 miles and could see what appeared to be a river (but every thing looked like a river), then we saw a "road closed" sign and beyond you could see the bridge completely under water. We turned what we thought was east and about 6 to 7 more miles the road ended into a lake with another bridge under water. We had a tricky time turning around with the truck on the back, but we did it and came all the way back to Crookston to find out that there was two State roads numbered 9.

6 pm and finally back on Highway 2 after going about 300 miles around. Even Interstate 29 was closed in areas. There were sections of 94 that were diked to keep water off of the highway. We have never seen such a disaster, and hope to never again. All day we've had high mountains of snow and water everywhere. We are now parked at a big truck stop and dinner is in the oven. Jerry is really tired. We are at Minot, N. Dakota and it's about 30 degrees.

April 23rd, slept good, cool this morning and we are headed west on US 2, about 100 miles west of Minot, N.D. It has turned very cold and raining. Jerry is now trying to assist a truck driver who is broke down. In this area there is nothing, no houses, no services, just rolling hills with no growth. Just sage brush and tumble weed.

6:30 pm and stopped at a Lions Club Rest area in Chester, Montana, a real nice park. We stayed here 3 years ago. We went across the street to a VFW and sure enough two of the guys came up to Jerry and remembered him from 3 years ago. (I wonder what it was that they remembered) ha ha. We came back to the motor home and made supper. We saw our first antelope today. We have finally left the snow and flooded areas.

April 24<sup>th</sup> and we are in Kalispell, Montana at a really nice campground right in town. We did the laundry, Jerry grilled steaks outside and the showers felt really good. We had a wonderful day, left Chester at 7 am, rainy and cool day, the closer we got Glacier National Park the sun was out brightly and the snow covered mountains were breathtaking. The snow is piled high along the shoulders and the streams are fast and high.

8:30 am. Sun is bright and the temperature is going to be 60 degrees (quite a change). We are surrounded by the mountains as we sit here having coffee. We can look out our windows and it's like a picture. We are going to stock up on supplies before heading for Canada tomorrow. We are really enjoying our trip and wish each and every one of you could do this also.

April 26<sup>th,</sup> and heading north on 93 out of Kalispell. It is a bright, sunny and cool morning and we'll be in Canada within the hour and then head for the National Parks of Kootenay, Yoho, Banff and Jasper. The mountains are covered with snow and some ice still on the lakes. This area is very mountainous with big cedar trees. So far we've seen a dog sled team and 2 deer.

9 pm and stopped for the night at the Jasper train station parking lot (we've stayed here many times). Had a wonderful trip through the parks, started with no snow and ended with tons of snow. It is the first time that we didn't see any bears. Came upon a herd of elk right in the road, and as we sit here at the station they are feeding right outside within 10 feet and Brandy is about to lose it if they come any closer.

8 am had a good nights sleep and woke up to rain. We started out from Jasper and again for miles we saw herds of elk all over. We took Highway 40, north from Hinton to Grand Prairie. We ran into a snow storm, saw some reindeer and stopped at a rest area for a late breakfast and now the temperature is 47, and real windy.

11:30 and finally made it to Grand Prairie. It is still extremely windy and we are out of the mountains. 3 pm and we're having another adventure. We were approximately 5 miles from reaching Dawson Creek when we ran out of gas.....yes.....ran out of gas and that also explains why our generator wouldn't keep running. It won't run if the gas supply falls below a certain point. We knew it was low and we were trying to make Dawson Creek, funny thing is we just passed a gas station about a mile back. Jerry hitched a ride into town to get gas and Brandy and I are sitting is the motor home getting rocked back and forth by the traffic and wind.

6 pm and we're safe and sound in a Safeway Supper Market parking lot. We went in, did some more stocking up and will make a trip to the butcher shop in town to get steaks for our cook outs at Laird Hot Springs, where we will stay for 4 or 5 days depending on the weather. It continued to be extremely windy and about 50 degrees. It's hard to believe the growth that we've seen in this town since 1984. We are now 3 hours behind Georgia and it's still hard for us to adjust; our clock's still say 9:20 pm.

We woke up to a bright and sunny 39 degrees and went to our favorite bakery and now waiting for the butcher shop to open. We are 477 miles from Laird Hot Springs and hope to go at least 375 miles today and camp at Muncho Lake. The wind is still strong and coming out of the west. As we leave Dawson Creek we start at mile 0 of the Alaska Highway.

We continue to enjoy this trip, maybe more so because we don't plan on doing it again. We feel we need to explore the lower 48 states and find what treasures they hold. We continued on to Fort Nelson, road is good, fair amount of snow on shoulders yet. Brandy is taking an early nap so as to be alert later for animals.

Forget what I said about the roads. They are rough now and we have had a variation of weather with snow flurries on and off and temperatures dipping down as low as 32 degrees. We saw a coyote and several caribou. Gas prices up to 68.9 per liter and we can easily drop $100.00 and not even fill the tank.

CARIBOU

Just stopped for a break and went to use the microwave and it wouldn't work; how do people make it camping in a tent?

1pm and I'm sitting around a roaring camp fire writing this. We arrived at Laird River Hot Springs at 9 pm last night. We were fortunate to get a site. We had another wonderful day yesterday. Saw some stone sheep, and more caribou. We ran into a few bad road sections. There is still snow here in the park. We went for a soak in the hot springs…..felt great!!!! The sun is out, but remains cool. We did eat lunch outside and Jerry's camp fires always keep you warm.

We plan on staying here until May 2$^{nd}$, just soaking in the springs and relaxing. It's steaks on the fire tonight. Brandy is taking a nap on the picnic table…snug in her blanket.

CAMP SITE AT LAIRD RIVER HOT SPRINGS

RED GOING FOR A SOAK IN THE HOT SPRINGS

April 30th, slept late, it's a little warmer…48 degrees. Jerry has been up, made coffee and tore the microwave out and we will replace it when we get to Anchorage. We saw our first moose while coming back from the springs.

May 2nd, and we are on the road again. We got up to ice on the truck windshield. Stopped for gas and coffee at the campground lodge…$6.78 for 2 cups and a quart thermos (won't do that again). The road is rough; we saw two buffalo along side of the road. Laird River is all ice. Sun is peeking through the clouds as we head for Whitehorse which is 400 miles down the road.

We came through Watson Lake and stopped for gas at 70.9 per liter…that really hurts when you are filling an 80 gallon tank.

WATSON LAKE FAMOUS SIGN VILLAGE

We stopped outside of town and made breakfast and now on terrible roads, all gravel and holes. We still have snow and the motor home, truck and boat are so dirty, it is difficult to tell the original color. No bath for them until Anchorage.

May 3rd and here we are in Whitehorse in a park overlooking the city and the Yukon River. Yesterday was beautiful again, cold but sunny. We went to the Canadian Legion last night to see our friend "Hank Karr" play…no luck as he had played the last three weeks and took this weekend off. He is going to be at the local trade fair that is on this week, so after getting the laundry done we will look him up.

No luck missed Hank again. Did laundry. Washers $2.00 and dryers $1.50. We're going to have to wear our clothes longer. Whitehorse is a city surrounded by mountains (now covered with snow). Even the Yukon River is partly covered with ice.

May 4th and we left Whitehorse at 8:30 am and just came through Haines Junction, getting colder and more snow as we get closer to Kluane Lake. We've seen 2 snow shoe rabbits, 2 prairie dogs and 1 porcupine.

2:30 pm and just drove through the roughest roads yet, lots of construction and rocks. Both of the lights on the truck got smashed out and we had about 40 miles before we finally got to smoother roads. We did see 2 moose in a pond and saw our first grizzly. I noticed this dark figure about 150 yards off the road in a marsh like area, the closer we got, and sure enough it stood on his hind legs and was moving his jaw in a fast motion. It's really exciting to see them stand and look at you.

We came through US Customs and lost another hour. The temperature is 50 degrees and has been sunny all day. We will be in Tok, Alaska in a couple of hours.

8:30 pm, and we are now in Tok. We went out to eat and now watching TV and just relaxing. We are in an RV Park with electric hook up, but no water as it's frozen yet. Brandy has crashed, she has had enough of rough roads and today was the worst yet.

Woke up to rain during the night and now it is cloudy and cool. We've been traveling three weeks now and today we'll head for Anchorage and spend a few days getting supplies for the summer in Homer. Oh yes! We thought once we got to Alaska the price of gas would go down….wrong. The gas in Tok was $158.9 to $161.90 per gallon.

We stopped at King Mountain State Park in the Matanuska Valley, about 25 miles from Palmer and 65 miles from Anchorage. Gas isn't the only thing that has gone up. We have paid $75.00 a year for the annual State Park Sticker and this year it is $200.00, so we will take advantage of every State Park that we can. It has been

184

an unusual day, weather wise. We started out with rain and went through pure winter and now it is 52 degrees in this valley by the Matanuska River. The roads have been absolutely terrible, with lots of frost heaves and when you're pulling a truck behind, you can't go to fast. We saw one moose in our 275 mile drive. We just came back from chipping ice in the river for our cooler.

Today is a beautiful, sunny day and warm here in the valley. We have the park all to ourselves and went for a walk along the river bank. I'm getting quite a collection of all the different types of pine cones. This park is nestled in among the pine trees and across the river the mountain goes straight up from the river bank.

May 7th and now were camped in the Wal-Mart parking lot. We did a lot of stocking up yesterday, including a new microwave and we'd better stop buying or we won't be able to move this vehicle down the road. We still need to buy a smoker for doing our salmon and then start down the Seward Highway towards Homer with stops along the way. Right now we are stopped for gas at $131.9 and that's a positive improvement.

To those of you who have made this trip before....they discourage parking at the Anchorage Wal-Mart. There must have been 10 or more motor homes in the lot at 9:30 am and the manager came knocking at our door to inquire how long we would be there. We had only been there for a few minutes. Remember this is a 24 hour Wal-Mart. I would question the lack of PR on his part, especially considering how much money the tourist spends.

We finished our shopping in Anchorage, boots, fish net, smoker and other fishing gear. Now we are at Morgan's Landing (State Park) approximately 85 miles north of Homer. We had heard last year that a lot of things had changed here and they sure have. We have been coming to this park since 1989, when it had no designated sites and then 4 years ago they did major revamping and turned the former fish camp into a State campground which greatly limited the number of campers. The campground sits high above the Kenai River and this is the number one river for fishing salmon (in my opinion) in all of Alaska. Now in order to control and limit the fisherman, they have fenced off all access to the river banks and only have a limited number of areas that you can fish (off wooden platforms). The whole purpose...so they say, is to stop river bank erosion and to increase the fish population. We are so glad that we started to come here years ago, because we sure have seen changes over the years (some good and some not). This has always been a favorite fishing spot of ours so we'll hope for the best when the fish run here in mid July.

FISH PLATFORMS ON THE KENAI RIVER

We were cooking steaks over the camp grill and all of a sudden I heard the snapping of nearby branches. Startled, I looked up to see a huge moose. Brandy got a sore throat from barking so much. The moose paid no attention to her barking and just kept on grazing on the foliage.

Tomorrow we head for Soldotna for fishing license, haircuts, wash job for the vehicles and stop to check out the various state parks for July and August fishing. Then it's on to the Kenai Moose Lodge for some R & R and to see old friends. Earlier we walked down to the river and to our old fishing spots with the changes mentioned. There were signs posted as to recent grizzly visits to the area and we kept a close look out.

Spent the day in Soldotna with all our various "must do list" and then continued down the peninsula to Johnson Lake State Park where we will stay and try our luck with fishing for rainbow trout.

Our site here is right on the lake. We took the boat out and saw a couple of trout, but no luck. We looked for wood and Jerry found a felled tree which made a great fire. Today we slept in late, it's the first day that we've had cold and on and off rain for quite some time. Jerry slept most of the day and I read Danielle Steel's book *Going Home*. There are a lot of campers here, even in spite of the weather.

Happy Mother's Day, got a beautiful card from Jerry. Sun is trying its best to peek out, but continues to rain on and off. We can see all kinds of trout, but they won't bite. We packed up the boat and will leave for Homer tomorrow.

May 12th, and now back in Homer. We are camped on the Spit and our view is snow covered mountains and glaciers and to our left is Kachemak Bay and to our right the Cook Inlet. Right ahead is the fishing harbor with its hundreds of boats, commercial as well as personal watercraft. We will stay here till around the 16th of June and hopefully catch our limit of King Salmon to smoke and can. We also look forward to visiting with old friends and once again I will work at the hospital here.

HOMER BOAT HARBOR

Spent yesterday banking, checking in with the post office for forwarded mail and went up to the hospital to see old friends and co-workers to let them know I'm available for work. It was really great to see people that I've worked with since 1989. Our friends Tom and Jean came down for a visit to catch up on old times; great to see them. We had seen Tom in December of last year when he came to see us and again in February in Florida.

Today our friend Ferris Brown arrived from our town in Georgia (Blairsville). He has property north of Fairbanks and he will be fishing here till the first of the month. The sun is out brightly, but it has rained for the past two days. The Spit is slowly filling up with campers; all anticipating the arrival of the King Salmon.

What a night, in all our years of traveling, we have never been in such winds. It blew all night, and still is up, blowing in off the ocean and hitting us sideways in the motor home.

Later in the day, the wind finally calmed down, but remains cool. As I sit here I watch the numerous young people pitch tents across the road on the beach of Cook Inlet. The beaches are not what you think of when you hear of a beach. Here they are glacier sand and rock. I can see eagles soaring overhead and watch them when they swoop down to fish and then land to eat their catch. It's interesting to watch the fishing boats as they return to the harbor with hopefully a good days catch.

May 23$^{rd}$ and the first Kings are in the fishing hole on the Spit and Jerry is down trying his luck and I'm making plans to return to work tomorrow.

VARIOUS TOURIST SHOPS ON THE SPIT

Today we are just acting like regular tourists, its fun to explore all the little shops on the Spit. We tried fishing again and the closest we came to a fish, was when Jerry netted one for someone else.

Remember a while back when we had to replace the microwave? Well now the TV bit the dust last night. It was 8 years old so now we'll buy a combination VCR/TV.

Jerry got up at 5 am and went razor clamming and came back empty handed. I had chores to get done; wash the dog, laundry and a hair cut. I now have a beeper that the hospital provided and maybe it wasn't such a good idea. I got called times 2 today, and I'm already on the schedule for tomorrow.

May 22<sup>nd</sup> and back to the fishing hole. We saw 3 salmon being caught, but none for us. It now stays light until midnight.

May 23<sup>rd</sup> and a very full day again. I worked the 7 am to 3 pm shift and started the morning with 3 major trauma victims. Three male patients all 21 to 28 years old involved in a one car accident that ran off the road and hit an embankment. All were stabilized and transferred by air to Anchorage.

Today we met Tom and Jean for breakfast and then went out 12 miles in the Cook Inlet for halibut fishing. It was a perfect warm and sunny day with absolute calm waters (rare here). We came back with our quota of 8 halibut and 6 cod. I also hooked into a sting ray and it gave me a real fight before getting it off my hook. We returned home and had a feast of deep fried halibut.

Our friend Ferris, left for Valdez and we spent the day as typical tourists again.

Memorial Day; and spent it at Tom and Jeans annual picnic with BBQ ribs and chicken. It was nice to see all the people that we have met over the years. We tried fishing later in the day and still no luck.

May 28<sup>th</sup> and finally I got a king on and what a fight, only to lose it due to it being snagged. I worked last night and on the way home came upon Mother Moose out for a stroll with her two tiny babies.

Mother Nature is experiencing a tragic loss of the death of spruce trees due to the "spruce beetle." A large area has turned brown and is a great fire danger too! The area includes almost the entire Kenai Peninsula and is changing the beautiful landscape. The threat of lightning and resulting possibility of fires is scary.

Back to the fishing hole and after two hours of casting, Jerry finally landed a 20 pound king and needless to say he was excited. He also caught one the following day, so today is canning day and we got 2 and ½ cases of ½ pint jars.

June 7<sup>th</sup> and the summer is going by to fast. I worked 7A to 7P, couldn't say no, they are so short staffed. I had the beeper turned off, but they know where we are parked. It sure is staying light long after midnight now and it is always so strange to go to bed when it is still light out. Today I'm making halibut chowder and rhubarb pie. Jean brought rhubarb from her yard. It's raining out, and a good day to catch up on cleaning, letter writing, laundry and rest.

June 8th, and it is another rainy day and cool. We went to the local entertainment spots. We visited three local bars. The first one the band playing was not good (putting in nicely), the second one, the band was real good, but the speakers didn't work. The third one played "old folks music". One can't afford to get drunk here. Beer by the glass is $3.50 and mixed drinks in small glasses range from $4.00 and up.

The fishing hole is full of anxious anglers and the whole town is packed with tourists like us. We leave for the Russian River on the 18th staying through the 26th and when we return we are booked into the Ocean View RV Park till the 18th of July.

Got a letter from our friends, Jack and Linda from Massachusetts, and they will fly into Anchorage July 23rd and we will fish with them at Morgan's July 26th to the 30th.

We took a change in our usual schedule and went to Soldotna to do some shopping and play bingo. Jerry won $60.00 but zero for me. Jerry got his fishing rod replaced after it broke while trying to land a big fish. It has rained most of the past 4 days.

June 15th; Father's Day. I made Jerry's favorite foods, mashed potatoes with garlic, roast pork with mushrooms and pumpkin pie. Come Wednesday, we will be going back to the Russian River and hope to get a lot of fish.

I worked the 3 to 11 shift last night. I started out in the ER and when the ER slowed down I ended up working in the ICU. In this small hospital everyone is expected to function in most of the units.

June 18th, 7 pm and here we sit at Fred Meyer's parking lot in Soldotna. We left Homer at 10:30 this morning. We drove to Kenai and had lunch at the Moose Lodge, then went to K-Mart to stock up on some items. So now we will sit here and wait till midnight and then travel the 50 to 60 miles to the Russian River. Over the years we've found that if we go in really late the chances are better to get a site to park.

June 19th at 11:30 am what a night last nigh! We left Fred Meyers at midnight and headed for the river. It was an absolutely beautiful night for the drive. The sky was clear as we wound our way through the mountains and the moon cast a luminous glow on the landscape. We saw another moose and 2 more porcupines. When we arrived at the river we were shocked! The parking lot was almost filled to the hilt and it probably holds 60 to 70 vehicles, plus the overflow was "over flowing", but we managed to get the best spot there was. We parked in the very end lot, with no one to our right and woods to our back. Usually you are packed in so tightly it can be difficult to open your door. We even had room for the truck, and to top it off, the only water pump in the entire park was no more than 20 feet away. We were still awake at 2:30 am still digesting our luck in finding a spot. Across the river there were fishermen shoulder to shoulder, the sockeye run is so strong that fish and game has increased the daily limit from 3 to 6 fish per person. The sanctuary was also opened. We finally went to bed at 3:30 am and it still wasn't dark.

When we were at Fred Meyers, we could have bought the fish for $2.09 a pound, but instead we fight the crowd, pay $11.00 a day to park (no facilities), $4.00 per person to ride the water ferry to the other side of the river to fish shoulder to shoulder and to boot drive over 5000 miles to get here. Is there something wrong with us? We are going to be here till the 26th, so we'll take our time getting to the fish. As I sit here and write, I watch the continuous line of vehicles hoping to get a spot, if one vehicle goes out, they let one in, and otherwise you may be in line for hours. We did that experience back a few years and got smart and came in the wee hours of the morning.

RUSSIAN RIVER PARKING LOT

June 20th, 8 pm-Just came back after 8 hours of fishing....I finally landed 2 after losing 12-"fish on/fish off". Jerry got 0, but had on equally as many as I. The river is extremely swift and to stand on slippery rocks in the fast current takes a lot out of you. The fish appear bigger than years before, this run is averaging 6 to 10 pounds, but with the strong current it feels like 25 to 30 pounds.

We didn't fish yesterday as it rained hard all day. Today is nicer, but rained a little in the afternoon. Being here is like being is a multi cultural gathering, Germans, Japanese, Italians and other nationalities present. So far most everyone is very tolerant of the many times that your lines get tangled. Remember you are fishing shoulder to shoulder and it pays to be in rhythm. We sometimes wonder if maybe we should be fishing in calmer waters – say maybe in a boat in warm weather.

June 22nd and back at Fred Meyers. We arrived here around 2 am from the river. We needed to fill with water, dump sewer and take showers. There were so many people at the river; it's difficult to explain how hundreds of "would be fishermen" could assemble at an area with one thought in mind "kill those fish". How any fish gets up stream to spawn is beyond me.

WAITING TO GET ON THE FERRY

The area that was hot for fishing on Friday was stone cold on Saturday. So maybe when we go back tonight we'll have a better day tomorrow. We hope it will be less busy, as the Anchorage people will have to go back to the city. Today it is bright, sunny and in the 70's.

7 pm and we are still at Fred Meyers along with 50 or 60 other RV's. Jerry just cooked a steak outside and would you believe it? - Thunder! They rarely have thunder here and this is the 2nd time this year that we have heard it. The clouds look more like Florida clouds and here we sit awaiting the rain. We have a perfect parking spot here in this mass of vehicles. Our door faces the curb and we have a sloping hill with flowers and grass and very private. To our left is the parking lot, the store and all the other vehicles. It's fun to walk around and visit with other RVers. They are from all over. We'll get some sleep, set the alarm for 1 am and drive back down to the river for 3 more days of –hopefully-fish.

THE RUSSIAN RIVER FERRY

Yesterday was the best fishing we've ever had. We drove back to the river and it was packed again and I thought "oh no", and would you believe it there was one space right on the river side for a large motor home and one little space down a bit for the truck. Our view is spectacular as we are 50 feet back from the river and have a bird's eye view of the fishermen, mountains and all the people coming and going with their fish.

THE VIEW FROM OUR MOTOR HOME

Our fishing day started at 11am and we went back to our favorite spot across the river. Fishing action started with a bang! Right away I got 2 on and 2 off, with eventually getting 2 and then none for several hours. At 4 pm they really started running. We lost more than we could count. There was real comedy too! Jerry was after one of my fish to net and he got turned around with the fish going everywhere and Jerry is desperately trying to net a fish close to shore, except the fish he was chasing was already on a stringer! No stopping him either, he was convinced that it was the right fish and meanwhile I'm still fighting it in the strong current.

It's a fishing frenzy when several fish are on at the same time. Jerry fell in the strong current three times while trying to net or land a fish, I fell once on the slippery rocks. The current is extremely strong and you have to get out in the river about 6 to 8 feet to be in line with all the others.

THE FAMOUS SOCKEYE SALMON

Jerry was taking a nature break when I got another fish on. The guy next to me netted it. I got it to shore and out of the net, I whacked it on the head a few times, and thought is was finished and wrong! It slithered away from my grasp and out in the river again. Jerry finally gave me a time limit, we leave the river at 9 pm- I had taken one break in 10 hours and could have stood there for 10 more. The night ended with 7 fish for me and sorry to say, 0 for Jerry. He was kept busy restringing poles, netting fish and putting up with my fishing addiction. I truly love fishing here better than the slots in Las Vegas. The problem is that no other place in the world that I know of has fishing like this.

Today is canning day and rest up for more fishing tomorrow. So far we have the first load (16 jars) coming out of the pressure cooker and 16 more to go in and I'm still packing jars. We will probably get 4 ½ cases out of 9 fish. Hopefully the fish caught tomorrow will go back to Homer for Jerry to smoke.

Jerry recognized a guy by the name of "Moose" that we've fished with for years at Morgan's Landing. Moose is in his 80's and he had already gotten his limit of 6 fish.

June 25th and what a day we've had. We caught 7 more fish and I took my annual bath in the river. I changed clothes and fell in again! – Oh well – such is the life of the fisherwoman.

Back in Homer and now at Ocean View RV Park. We are high on a bluff overlooking the Kachemak Bay and Cook Inlet with the mountains with glaciers in the background.

We truly do live in a strange world. We met a strange person at Fred Myers before coming back to Homer. We were in the parking lot, hooking up our truck behind the motor home and this guy came over, stood for a few seconds, and then asked "are you going to pull that truck?, Jerry wanted to say – No! We're going to drive in reverse and pull the motor home!"

Today is smoking day, and it is quite a process. First you cut the fish in pieces, brine it for 10 hours and then dry in for several hours and then smoke for 5 to 6 hours. Jerry has Bud to thank for his teaching him how to smoke fish.

July 1st and it is Brandy's birthday. She is 5 years old. Her treat today is her favorite trip to McDonalds for an ice cream cone. (Yes – she is spoiled). A thick layer of fog covers part of the bay, but it remains sunny and warm. The campground here is full with the 4th of July coming soon. We will be going to the annual Elks party.

My shifts at work have been extremely busy lately. Last night I worked the 3 to 11 shift and got home at 1:30 am. The long night included two cardiac arrests along with numerous other patients.

They opened up snagging of Kings in the fishing hole on the Spit. This is one kind of fishing that we don't partake in. The snagging hook consists of a heavy hook with multiple barbs on it and the anglers throw it wildly in hopes of snagging the big King Salmon. The King is at the end of its life cycle and is already turning a red color. The fishing hole will be closed to snagging next week to await the arrival of the second run of Kings, which will be even larger (30 to 40 pounds).

The past two weeks has not been too healthy for several people. A lot of tragic accidents have happened in Alaska. Fourteen members of a mountain climbing team fell 1000 ft., killing 2 and injuring the rest. A cardiologist drowned in a white water accident. Three airplanes went down, with a total loss of 12 people, mostly tourists. A man was mauled and died later from a grizzly attack. Two kids were killed from an ATV accident. Makes you really appreciate life.

July 8th and I work 3 to 11. It is a beautiful, sunny day. It seems strange to see people in T-shirts and shorts (in Alaska). Jean brought over some rhubarb and I did up 32 cups and put it the freezer.

July 9th and yup! Another beautiful day in Alaska! I worked 3 to 11 and very busy in the ER. I got home at 12:30 am and the beeper went off at 6:30 am to see if I'd work 7 to 3 today- I finally said no!! Today is laundry, grocery shopping and tomorrow were having Tom and Jean over for steaks and I'll make a birthday cake for Tom's 53rd birthday. The tide is way out and where we are parked we can see the waves splash along the shore line. The fireweed is really out now, with its bright crimson flowers.

July 10th. We slept late. Went to see Hobo Jim entertain. He is playing at Alice's Palace, one of the local night spots in Homer. Hobo Jim is quite famous in Alaska and as we found out, also in the lower 48 and in Europe. We've seen him in previous years, but last night he came over to our table and talked with us. He has written many songs, not only for himself, but also for more well known artists, such as Anne Murray, Garth Brooks and others. He was at Mackinaw Island, Michigan several weeks ago and in the winter has a studio in Nashville, Tennessee.

Today is the first cloudy day in weeks and wouldn't you know it looks like rain and were planning on doing steaks outside. The second run of Kings has yet to come in to the fishing hole, so we're in a "fishing hold". The TV has been announcing on the news the danger of bears and guess where? – Yup – the Russian River. Last nights news stated and showed the mother grizzly and her 2 cubs driving anglers out of the river. They had to kill one grizzly at the cabin by the ferry. Hope they get them under control before next week when we are scheduled to go back.

The Sockeye Salmon are also slow coming into the Kenai as the waters are to warm.

We went to Jose's grand opening (Mexican Restaurant). The restaurant had just been remodeled and had a great party with authentic Mexican band.

Our time is winding down in Homer and it is sad to think we are spending our last few days here, but we've gained unforgettable memories of our many trips here and learned experiences that couldn't be achieved anywhere else in the world.

July 15th and one can hardly see the mountains from all the smoke from wild fires in the interior Alaska. Tomorrow we leave for Morgan's Landing.

July 17th and camp is all set up. The fish are running. We walked down to the river (about ½ to ¾ mile) to check out the activity. Fish are being brought in, so it should be a fun week. Brandy is busy checking out the moose droppings.

Oh what a day we had yesterday. It was beautiful weather and we did get fish! The limit was 6 per person and it took us only 5 hours to get 10 fish. The getting was easy, hauling them up the hill and back to camp was the hard work. Jerry had to make a trip to Soldotna to get more jars, ice and tackle. Then the work of canning begins. 80,000 fish went through the counter at Soldotna yesterday.

July 23rd and we are in camp again (Morgan's) We had to leave and be out for one day before we could come back in for 6 more days. I got up at 8 am and drove the pickup to Morgan's from Soldotna, with a plan that if I didn't return in an hour or so, Jerry would assume that I got a site and then he would bring the motor home, it's a really rough road from the highway back to Morgan's and not one to make needlessly with the motor home. I found only 3 sites available, and really none of which were really to my liking, but I slid into one and decided I couldn't be too fussy. I waited for Jerry to come and site 6 opened up and it's a great site closer to the path that leads down to the river, so now we're all set up for another 6 days of camping and fishing.

Our site is on a bluff and when we walk out a few feet, we can see the Kenai River below. We are surrounded by spruce trees and brightly colored fireweed. The silence of the area is broken with the song of birds, and once in a while the cry of a distant loon. Every now and then the noise of a jet can be heard to remind you that you are still not far from the commercial world.

I'm trying a new way of doing salmon tonight. Marinate the steaks in lemon juice, soy sauce, sesame oil and pepper overnight and then grill for 8 minutes on each side. I'll let you know how it turns out!

July 28th, the salmon was delicious! We took a day off from fishing and traveled to Seward, which had really grown since we were there 6 or 7 years ago.

The town was packed with tourists. Seward sits overlooking Resurrection Bay, a harbor that leads out to the Pacific Ocean. Cruise ships were in port and the harbor was filled with boats of every description.

We stopped at Exit Glacier, perhaps one of the most beautiful and approachable glaciers that we've ever seen. There are easy paths to hike that make it accessible to almost everyone. On the way back to Morgan's the traffic was heavy with all the traffic heading north to Anchorage. There is only one road between Anchorage and Homer and it keeps one on guard for the entire 240 mile trip. There were a few fishermen in the river, but it would appear that the run is almost over. The campground is only half full now. I guess we are lucky at the fish we have gotten so far.

The bears are really active again. They are driving people out of the river and stealing fish. Jerry and I were sitting outside our motor home about 5 pm and all of a sudden we heard this loud "roar" or "growl" from a bear at the end of the campground, so we are really alert.

July 29th and the bears are so aggressive that night fishing as been banned. The fish supply is so low that the bears aren't getting their quota either.

August 2nd. I worked 7A to 4P, very busy. I'm on call tomorrow, off the next 2 days and then work one more shift and that's it. I will miss all! And I'm sure I will get tearful with goodbyes and the thought that I may never see the staff here again. Life's journey can be sad in many ways, but I'll treasure the memories.

This is our last full day in Homer. The weather is absolutely beautiful and the mountains and the bay are picturesque. It will be sad to leave here, but look forward to our new adventures over the next month in our journey home.

SEAFARER'S MEMORIAL

The Seafarer's Memorial is in tribute to all those who have died while working on the high seas.

## MT. REDOUBT ~ JUST ONE OF MANY VOLCANOES ACROSS COOK INLET

The more north we head the fireweed has almost lost all of its flowers and the aspen trees are taking on their fall yellow color. The highway runs along side of Cook Inlet and the views of the water and volcanoes is breathtaking. Traffic is very heavy (100 miles south of Anchorage) with anglers heading to Seward for the Silver Salmon Derby.

It is so different from the spring, now there are only small patches of snow visible on the mountain peaks and the rest is a lush green.

August 10th, and we are camped at Nancy Lake, north of Wasilla, Alaska. The park is 6.5 miles inland from the Parks Highway, on the worst washboard road that you can imagine. Our site is on a lake in the heart of primitive bush country-quite a contrast from parking at Wal-Mart last night. The only noise we heard was the cry of the elk in the distance.

We woke up to rain and at this rate we will never get a glimpse of Mt. Denali. This is the kind of weather you get before it turns to snow and it usually snows in August.

6 pm and here we are – camped along the Parks Highway at McKinley View Campground, which is about 7 miles from the entrance to Denali (remember that there are two names for the mountain) Mt. McKinley and Mt. Denali.

We never did see the mountain, and headed on to Fairbanks. The city has really grown since our last visit. We acted like a typical tourist and visited several well known areas; AlaskaLand (a combination of arts, crafts and history of the area). And the next day headed for the "North Pole" – Santa Claus Land, which has a year around one stop tourist "must see" Christmas Shop, with every thing for the Christmas season that one would want.

The next day we started out for Tok, Alaska. We saw a full grown bull moose right along the side of the road. The weather is getting warmer. We came through Delta Junction that was flooded in a lot of areas, with roads almost entirely washed out. We were going to camp at Moon Lake (25 miles west of Tok), but the park was closed due to bears in area! We continued to the State Park 6 miles east of Tok, on the Tok River. We met 3 couples that we met at Morgan's, again at Fairbanks and now here. Two of the couples are from Australia and one couple from British Columbia. The trees haven't started to turn here yet and no snow on these mountains, but we have seen several flocks of geese heading south.

August 15th is a warm, sunny day. We drove 200 miles to "Skully's" to see the famous "Burl Man", who creates gifts made from burl wood. He made our walking sticks and we are going to need them to lose the extra pounds we've gained.

We drove on another 70 to 80 miles and stopped at a gravel pit for the night. We had the scare of our lives. We were out walking and Brandy was not on her leash. All of a sudden I saw a movement and there 150 feet away was a coyote with a fixed stare on Brandy. Jerry was in the motor home and I yelled to him to open the door and with one eye on the dog and the other eye on the coyote I moved toward the door and fortunate for Brandy she came when called, all the while the coyote stood in a trance. After getting Brandy in the coach, Jerry and I took some video footage as Jerry is chasing the beast off, as for Brandy, she will be on a leash.

8 am the next day, a beautiful, clear, cold morning. The coyote howled on and off before we went to bed and Brandy wanted to go play with the "doggie". We are about 150 miles from Whitehorse and then another 100 miles south to Skagway,

where we will spend a couple of days. This is a beautiful mountainous area, but here too the spruce trees are all dying from the "spruce beetle disease."

3:30 pm and we arrived in Skagway. I thought we had seen the most beautiful places before, but we think this is it! We drove 96 miles south from Whitehorse and went through what appeared a geological trip around the world. We went through an area of sand dunes and then into an area of what appeared as though a volcano had erupted and threw rocks all over of every size. We then descended eleven and one half miles into a steep gorge surrounded by emerald green water, glaciers and snow covered mountains. It is so beautiful here it makes one wonder why this hasn't been preserved into a national park. The brakes on the motor home got to smelling very hot (remember we are pulling a pickup behind). This was a very steep grade and one time Jerry pulled over to let the brakes cool off. He got out to check everything and discovered a gas hose by the engine was pouring out gas. We finally limped into the village that is nestled in the narrow gorge. We found our campground and Jerry replaced the hose (we were lucky).

The campground overlooks the harbor and 3 cruise ships are in town. The streets are lined with old, well preserved buildings from the gold rush days. A shopper's paradise waits. The history of the gold rush days is well preserved. You can take a 3 hour train to the top of White Pass on the Chilkoot Trail. We are right on the edge of town, so we can walk to everything. We walked to a restaurant for breakfast and later shopped till we dropped. We then drove to the head of the Chilkoot Trail and then drove back up the steep climb out of the gorge to take pictures of the beautiful scenery that we had passed earlier.

SKAGWAY HARBOR

We met a girl from Traverse City, Michigan who knew Jerry's sister and brother-in-law. She also told us that they closed Laird River Hot Springs due to a bear killing 2 people and injuring several others before being shot. For those of you who have been there, it happened on the board walk by the hanging gardens.

## RED SHOPPING IN SKAGWAY

We left Skagway after wonderful memories and plans to return again. We are now on the shore of Teslin Lake, which is about 50 miles long. Jerry has a great camp fire and we are just relaxing.

August 19th, 7:30 pm and here we sit, camped at Laird Hot Spring, they just reopened late this after noon. All the talk along the route was that it was still closed. The ranger filled us in on what happened, apparently a 250 pound black bear was stalking a 12 or 13 year old child and attacked her. When her 38 year old mother came to her defense she was killed as well as another 57 year old man. The child and a 20 year old male were injured. The lower spring is open, but the boardwalk to the upper spring is closed. We were very careful and took our pepper spray with us.

August 21st and now we are in Dawson Creek. The tragedy took away from the good times we usually had at the springs. Our trip continues towards home by way of Idaho and US 93 with plans to unhook the truck to go over the 7264 ft. pass, then we head south to the Salmon River. So you see our adventure goes on! We've got to get these back roads out of our system if we go to a bigger unit. We made the pass without difficulty and now we have left the tumble weed and bareness and traded it for a thick forest of ponderosa pine. There is construction ahead, so we must await a "pilot car" to take us about 14 miles down the gorge. We are deep in the Rocky Mountains and heading for Salmon, Idaho.

We have been following the beautiful Salmon River for several hours. The river is fast and clear.

6 pm, temp is still 80 degrees, and we are now at a beautiful campground in Sun Valley, Idaho. Our site is on the river with lush grass at every site and an in-ground fire pit. Sun Valley is a quaint town with lots of shopping for the "rich and famous". The houses in this town are out of the *Rich and Famous* too! I've never seen such pads. We came by the ski slopes and now we can say we've been to Sun Valley, Idaho, too.

From here we will speed up our journey towards home and dream of making the trip to Alaska "One more time".

# ELMO

In September of 1998, we were sent a gift (only we didn't see it as such). We were busy with fall cleaning when we first heard a "meow". Upon further investigation, we discovered this very skinny, sad looking and frightened cat at our back door. It ran away a short distance, when we opened the door and Jerry was convinced it was "Elsa", a cat that also found her way to our door several years earlier. We had given Elsa to our electrician and had heard that she had disappeared from her new home, and Jerry was convinced that she had come the 20 miles to return here. With some coaxing with food the cat came and devoured the plate of food and with that we were now blessed with its presence.

After a few days the cat would come closer and a bond of trust was slowly being established. Jerry was still convinced that it was Elsa, and it was only when I pointed out the difference in the anatomy as the cat was walking away, that he agreed that it wasn't Elsa. And so, Elsa is now "Elmo."

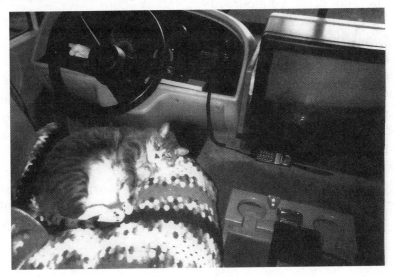

ELMO

Elmo became a limited member of the family. Brandy wasn't quite sure that this was entirely acceptable. Elmo accepted Brandy, leaving one to think that he was a family pet that shared his existence with a dog. Elmo was kept totally outside, as Jerry stated "No way, is that cat coming in the cabin". So it became an acceptable life for the cat. He had an outside self-feeder and plenty of water and he could come and go as he wanted.

In October we purchased another motor home, this time a 37' Southwind which was 4 years old. We felt true luxury now and started planning our next adventure.

Come November, the fall chill really set in and we decided we needed a little more warm weather and made plans to spend a few months in Florida. I took a 13 week contract in the Emergency Department of Brandon Regional Hospital, in Brandon, Florida. Brandon is due east of Tampa.

The planning was excitement, but the thought of leaving Elmo was very emotional to me. Jerry definitely was not going to allow a "cat" in the motor home. Our neighbor's, Al and Lois Green would be his adoptive grandparents to keep his food and water supply full until our return.

We left on December 5, 1998, and I was distraught in leaving Elmo behind. We came home for 4 days over New Years and when we drove in the drive way, Elmo came running to us with his familiar "meow". I was shocked to see the swelling over his left eye and with closer look realized it was a draining wound. We took him to the vet and was informed that he probably had gotten into a fight and now needed to be kept in the animal hospital for care of his wound and also that he needed to be neutered and have his required shots. We had no background on this cat so assumed that he never had any shots.

We brought him home the day before we had to return to Florida and Jerry allowed the cat to be in the warm cabin for only a short time. One of the hardest things I've ever had to do, was to put Elmo back out into the cold and drive off and leave him. Jerry had secretly hoped that he would run off long before this.

We returned home on March 16th and seeing Elmo as he once again ran up to greet us, was the greatest home coming ever. My feelings for this "gift" were very confusing to me; in as much as I really wasn't drawn to cats at all, but this was no ordinary cat. He is special.

Come November of 1999 and Elmo is still an outdoor cat. All of my coaxing met with deaf ears as far as Jerry was concerned. We made a trip to Michigan for Thanksgiving and when we returned Elmo was very sick. We made another trip to the vet and the diagnosis was pneumonia and another abscess on his chest, due to another fight. This time Jerry gave in and Elmo was finally given a warm environment. Even the vet stated that she had never seen such a special cat. He is so docile and always allowed his medicine to be given and after a few days he even stood very still and allowed us to remove the stitches from his chest. And so it took over a year, but he finally won his place in the house.

Now we are ready to make another trip to Alaska, and yes, Elmo is going too! And once again he has proven to be so special. He adapted to motor home life like he had done it all his life, which once again makes us wonder what his background is. The vet thinks he is about 3 to 5 years old.

April 15, 2000, and we leave for our second home. The cabin has had many changes since 1997 and our life also is a constant change with many adventures. We leave in a larger more comfortable motor home and a new passenger on board.

ELMO

OUR CABIN

This year we travel in a 1994, 37 foot Southwind which has all the creature comforts.

Our first stop on this trip was in Kentucky. The foliage is out more here than at home, with an abundant amount of red bud trees in bloom. The weather is cloudy with small amount of rain now and then.

We stopped for the night at a rest area, just south of Cincinnati, Ohio, and it didn't take long to realize that we're right under the flight path with a jet passing over head every few minutes. Our first day was uneventful except for the excitement of watching Elmo react to his new environment. He goes wild with all the birds and the traffic doesn't faze him at all, in fact he will get up on the dash and is very curious about everything as we travel down the road at 65 miles an hour.

April 26. We left Michigan after visits with family. We took my mom out of the nursing home to the casino, which she really enjoyed and also took her out for Easter dinner.

We left Charlevoix and headed north to Alaska. We ran into a lot of snow in Michigan, and then it was 70 degrees in Minnesota. We spent our first night in a campground in Minnesota and left the next day for Minot, North Dakota. It turned cold and very windy with storm clouds to our west.

April 27th and we are in Montana, and it truly is "Big Sky Country". The landscape is rolling hills dotted with an occasional dwelling. Our goal for today is to reach Glacier National Park.

We spent last night in a rest area at 5800 feet in Glacier (the southern rim). Outside of Alaska, this to me is the most awesome wilderness area that one can visit for any close comparison. We are surrounded by mountains covered with snow and glaciers, the rest area was open, but just the parking area, bathrooms were still closed with approximately 5 feet of snow. Elmo had a field day with watching all the ravens.

We left the park and headed to Kalispell, Montana. We wound through the mountains and followed the rushing streams from the long winter run off. We will stay in Kalispell for a couple of days to catch up on laundry and stocking up on supplies before heading into Canada.

April 30th. We left Kalispell at 8 am. It is fairly clear and sunny with a temperature of 46 degrees. We stopped at the border near Eureka, Montana and entered Canada with the usual interrogation. Then we headed on to the National Parks of Kootany, Banff and Jasper. There was very little snow except for the summit before Athabathscan Glacier, and then there was tons of the white stuff. The only critters we saw were sheep and elk.

Now at 6:45 pm, we are sitting at the train station in Jasper, Alberta. It is one of our usual stops along the route. We usually see elk here, but none so far.

May 2nd. We arrived in Dawson Creek, British Columbia yesterday. We left the train station and drove on Highway 40 (230 miles) with services at the 125 mile marker. The highway winds up and down the mountains, some of which are quite steep. We started out with sun and had a snow storm about halfway through. We saw herds of elk and lots of deer. We are now at a campground in Dawson Creek and have already done our stocking up again, especially with our steaks for when we are at Laird Hot Springs.

The next day we saw caribou, moose, reindeer, coyote and one dead black bear. We encountered snow, sleet, gravel and mud and also a forest fire. Some of the lakes are open, but most are still frozen over. The roads are fair to good and a few travelers on the road. We welcomed the soothing waters of the hot spring after getting settled in our camp site. The whole trip is worth setting in the natural hot spring. This is the same spring where 2 people got killed by a bear in 1997, so it makes one very cautious and we carry pepper spray just in case. It is always interesting to visit with people at the springs, some are going to Alaska for the first time and you can see the excitement in their faces and it brings back memories of our first trip.

We started out for Whitehorse after it started snowing at the springs. A black bear crossed in front of us and it appeared to ignore our presence. The journey today will take us first to Watson Lake and then west to within 100 miles of Whitehorse where we spent the night at a rest area. It was a very cold night.

None of the campgrounds in Whitehorse are open. It has been too cold here; they can't turn on the water. We ended up staying behind a combination gas station, restaurant and motel. They gave us water, so we were able to take a shower. Tomorrow we head for Kluane Lake in the Yukon.

There is snow everywhere, more than we've ever had here. All the lakes are frozen over. Every trip that we have taken to Alaska has always been a surprise as to the varied weather that we encounter.

May 8th, and here we sit in Sam's parking lot in Anchorage. We traveled yesterday from Whitehorse to Tok, saw 2 coyotes, 2 porcupines and 1 big bobcat. Stopped at Scully's again, (the Burlwood Man) and had our usual toast and tea and a good visit with the locals. We continued on very rough roads to Tok and stayed at a campground where we did laundry, washed the vehicles and ourselves and ate dinner out at "Fast Eddy's". They give you so much food that we are having leftovers tonight. We came through more snow than we've ever seen on the trip from Tok to Anchorage. All of the camping areas were closed due to the cold weather. We saw 2 moose and a herd of reindeer. It is 45 degrees in Anchorage.

May 24th and catch up time in our ongoing adventure. We arrived in Homer on May 12th and got settled at the RV Resort that we will be at all summer. I made the mistake of letting the hospital know I was in town and my first day back at work was May 17th, and I've already put in 38 hours.

214

May 19th, was a little scary, a 5.7 earthquake, the hardest I've ever felt. I was at work and all agreed the hospital shook the most ever. The hospital sits right on a fault line. Jerry was in the motor home and it really shook him up too.

Our site here at Ocean View RV Park sits right on the high bank that overlooks Cook Inlet. Across the bay are the mountains with glaciers and it sure makes for quite a view. Across the inlet to the west, lie Mt. Augustine and also Cape Douglas as well as other small villages.

OUR SPOT FOR THE SUMMER

Eagles are so frequently in our picture and all kinds of water traffic, from fishing boats to huge oil tankers.

We were awakened by something walking outside the motor home at 11:45 pm and got up to see Mamma Moose and her twins walking across the campground, what a sight.

We have been doing our usual fishing and so far the kings have been running strong and we have caught 4 of them. The weather has been warm and we even have a little tan.

June 14th, we left Homer on the 12th and now we are at the Russian River for the first run of the sockeye salmon. The rules have really changed again. It now costs $7.00 a day to park the motor home (no hookups) and $5.00 for the truck and $5.00 for each person to ride the Ferry across the river to fish. The maximum stay is 24 hours, and then you have to leave. We'll be in this area till June 25th and then back to Homer for a couple of weeks before heading to Morgan's Landing for a week of fishing on the Kenai.

We reserved a site at River Quest Resort, right on the Kenai River and our site is no more than 150 feet away from the river.

We could only stay at Morgan's for 7 days, so decided to go this route and we were lucky to get the space at prime time.

This morning we were thrilled with the presence of a moose and her 2 babies grazing behind our coach.

June 20th and what a day we had yesterday. Jerry fell in love with a rod and reel that another guy had and was catching one fish after another so.......on Father's Day we went to Soldotna and he bought the "expensive fish killer", guaranteeing me that he would catch 6 fish the first day of use. Well guess what? After he fished for a while (with no luck), he wanted me to try the rod. The day ended with 6 fish for me and 0 for Jerry. Another thrill was across the river a mamma moose and her baby came out of the woods and walked along the shore. We canned 24 jars of salmon and fell into bed at 1:30 am totally wiped out.

I came close to dying....one way or another. I got foul hooked into a salmon and it took me stumbling down the river, almost lost Jerry's rod and reel and a native boy caught me before I could fall. If I had lost the rod, I surely would have been in deep trouble.

July 13th and here we are at River Quest Resort. We arrived here yesterday and the weather was absolutely beautiful. We met a lot of friendly people who stopped by to chat. One couple invited us to their home, which was right on the canal that leads to the river. They fixed a delicious steak dinner and we really enjoyed hearing about the area. They also had a cat (a 21 pound cat) with 7 toes on each of his front paws. The man was a retired veterinarian. Today the weather has changed to cool with rain. We have been gone from home for 3 months.

The past two days have been terrible. Jerry and I both have flu like symptoms; cramping, diarrhea, nausea, fever, chills and aching all over. Hope it is just the flu and not bad water. It has been raining off and on and expected to do so for the next few days. The salmon are starting to run, but we are to sick to care.

July 21$^{st}$. I got better and Jerry got worse with all the symptoms as listed before, plus very dizzy, low blood pressure and bloody diarrhea. I wanted him to get checked, but he wants to wait. The scare is that there has been an outbreak of E-coli here and he has all the symptoms except for the fever.

We arrived here on July 12$^{th}$ and it has rained everyday since the 13$^{th}$. Jack and Linda arrived two days ago and we spent almost all of our time visiting inside. We tried fishing once, Linda had one on for a short time and then today they left for Anchorage.

JACK AND LINDA AND A FEAST OF HALIBUT

July 28$^{th}$, the weather improved a little, but fish are not running. Jerry is still not feeling his best and now on top of everything else he has a terrible cold. I have been trying my luck at fishing alone. Yesterday I had 4 on and lost every one.

August 2$^{nd}$ and we decided to go into Seward to send out some fish for our neighbors back home. We are parked right on Resurrection Bay. It is still raining, foggy and cold. The next day we visited Exit Glacier on our way to Anchorage.

We left Anchorage yesterday and today we head for Hanes Junction and then on to Haines where we will put the truck, motor home and us on the ferry to Skagway.

DEZADEASH LAKE ON THE WAY TO HAINES


We went with all the other tourists that are here to a river a few miles from town to wait for the grizzly bears to come and feed on the salmon. Just at dusk, right on schedule, two teenage bears came to the river edge completely unafraid of all the people watching them and proceeded to do their fishing.

Tomorrow we leave here on the ferry to Skagway. We are looking forward to another visit to the quaint town.

August 11, and the trip on the ferry couldn't have been better. The weather was perfect. It took more time to load all the vehicles than it did to make the entire trip, which takes about one hour. Our camp site was right on the harbor, which made for perfect viewing of the cruise chips as they came into the harbor.

THE FERRY TO SKAGWAY FROM HAINES

WAITING TO BOARD

OUR MOTOR HOME WAITING TO LOAD

WATER TAXI

August 12th. We left Skagway and started our climb out of the gorge. Once again we camped at Laird River and will wind down before heading on towards home. To those of you that plan on making this trip, Laird River is a must stop. And so, we end this trip saga and who knows, we may make the trip "One more time."

# ALASKA "A WILDERNESS ESCAPE"

In April of 2002 we made another trip to Alaska. I didn't make a log of this year's adventure; instead I made notes of what I felt needed to be told. So this chapter will focus on many aspects of interest.

In 1942 the Alaska Highway was built, a joint venture between Canada and United States. The highway is 1500 miles long between Dawson Creek, British Columbia, and Fairbanks, Alaska. When we first started traveling the "Alcan", it was a winding route through an ever changing landscape, with long stretches between towns and or services. Every year we would encounter stretches of construction; where crews were either patching up, or in some areas, completely rebuilding the road. We have seen sections of the road made straighter. We have also seen guard rails completely exposed when the highway sank in the bog from the frost heaves. We remember when the Alcan was more of a challenge, and the trip more of interest, because you had to travel more slowly to encounter the curves and the ever present holes in the road. In our early trips, one could see the "mile posts", the usual white posts with black lettering to let you know the mile that you were at. You don't see the old mile posts now. Asphalt covers most of the road now, with occasional stretches of gravel in the construction areas. We have always found the road better in the spring, before the onslaught of the many travelers and far worse in late summer with dust and pot holes.

Dawson Creek is at mile 0 of the Alcan. We have always stopped here to stock up. The Butcher Shop is located in town and we recommend a stop here to buy the best meat around.

MILE 0    THE START OF THE ALCAN HIGHWAY
DAWSON CREEK, B.C.


We have never made a trip without meeting up with a "pilot car"; the car usually is a truck, whose purpose is to lead the way through a construction area with its caravan of vehicles following behind.

On the trip you will come upon services sparsely apart, which will consist of a gas station, restaurant, motel or cabins and a repair shop all or in part in a combined building.

The main towns are far apart and consist of Fort St. John, Fort Nelson, Watson Lake, Whitehorse and Tok where you turn south to get to Anchorage.

Laird River Hot Springs is between Fort Nelson and Watson Lake, and is always a favorite stop on our many trips.

LAIRD RIVER HOT SPRINGS

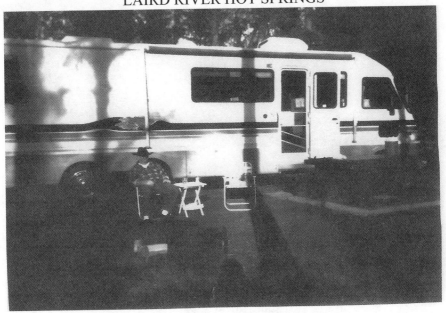

LAIRD IS SUCH A RESTFUL SPOT

Watson Lake is the home of the famous Sign Post Forest, and history states that it was started by a homesick soldier, who erected a sign pointing the way and stating the mileage to his hometown. Others copied him and are doing so still to this day.

Whitehorse is a modern city located on the shores of the Yukon River. It is also where you can go aboard the S.S. Klondike to learn more of the history of the city and the era of the steam ship.

The town of Tok lies at the junction of the Alaska Highway and the Glen Highway. The Alaska Highway continues on to Fairbanks and the Glen Highway leads to Anchorage. Fast Eddy's Restaurant is located here and is a great place to eat. You can also visit the Tok Visitor Center which includes wildlife displays and exhibits on the Gold Rush days and history of the building of the Alaska Highway. On the route to Anchorage is the spectacular Matanuska Glacier.

SNOW IN MAY

Anchorage is a large metropolitan city, modern in every way. It lies on the shores of Cook Inlet and bordered by mountains. Anchorage is 240 miles north of Homer. A visit to the Alaska Zoo is a must. Flowers of every color are prominent in all areas of the city. The long summer hours contribute to the vibrant colors. Anchorage is also known for the Iditarod Dog Sled Race to Nome in March. On a clear day you may catch a view of Mount McKinley some 237 miles away.

When you start out from Anchorage towards Homer, you head down the Kenai Peninsula and around the Turnagain Arm on the Seward Highway. The tides in this area can vary 30 feet or more within 6 hours. The mud flats of Turnagain Arms are like quicksand, and people have died when they ventured out on the flats, became mired in the quicksand and drown in the fast incoming tides. This part of the highway has seen much needed improvements. It has gone from a narrow two lane to a much wider road with many passing lanes. It was long known for having one of the highest numbers of traffic accidents. Along the entire route to Homer, the road has continued with improvements.

Refer to the *Milepost,* a valuable resource, to guide you along the way. Some of our favorites are: Portage Glacier and Whittier Tunnel that leads to Whittier.

PORTAGE GLACIER

When we first started coming to Alaska, Whittier could only be reached by train (with your vehicle), or just ride the train. Now, you can drive your vehicle through the tunnel. We took our van on the train through the tunnel in August of 1989. We then took a Ferry through Prince William Sound (sight of the oil spill) to Valdez. Valdez is home to the end of the pipe line and the oil terminal.

Along our route to Homer on the Seward highway out of Anchorage, we come to the junction of the Sterling Highway, and this is where we turn off to reach our favorite fishing spot in the whole world; the Kenai and Russian Rivers.

**RED**
**IN LINE TO CATCH THE FERRY AFTER A GOOD DAYS FISHING**

TIME TO CLEAN

FISH ARE IN THE CANNER

As we continue down the peninsula, we pass by Cooper Landing and Gwen's, a favorite restaurant. Once you are close to Soldotna, you will get a view of Mt. Redoubt, a volcano on the other side of the Cook Inlet. It is a spectacular sight.

As you continue on, you will come to Clam Gulch. From here to Homer you will have almost constant views of Cook Inlet and the volcanic peaks on the Alaska Peninsula. The views are truly a picture of unbelievable beauty of this wild country.

The village of Ninilchik is famous for its historic Russian Orthodox Church, which sits high on the hill overlooking Cook Inlet. During the negative tides there are hundreds digging for Razor Clams, including us. Deep Creek and the Ninilchik Rivers are over populated during the frenzy of fishing for King Salmon.

Homer is like our second home, and if it wasn't so far away (and a little warmer) we would live here. I don't think we could adapt to the long dark hours of winter either. Homer is situated on the north shore of Kachemak Bay at the easterly side of the mouth of Cook Inlet. The population of this small town increases by thousands during the summer months. The numbers include tourists as well as commercial fishermen and it has been said that Anchorage residents invade the area when their work week is over. The highway between the two cities is very dangerous on the weekend.

Homer is known as "The Halibut Capital of the World", and there are many charter services on the Spit. The Spit is famous for "The Fishing Hole", a man made lake with access to Kachemak Bay. The king salmon fry are released from the fishing hole and they return back in 4 or 5 years to complete their life cycle. It makes for very accessible fishing for the elusive king salmon.

## HOMER ALASKA

The community of Homer was first located at the end of the Spit. Homer came by its name from Homer Pennock, a miner and reported swindler from New York. History has it that "Homer" was chosen to be the name of the village by the sea, named after Homer Pennock. There is much to see and do around Homer. There is a variety of shops to explore; from art galleries to typical tourist shops. An abundant choice of restaurants to please everyone's appetite awaits you. The Pratt Museum is a must stop for the cultural history of the area and also exhibits that include wildlife and sea creatures.

Homer can be reached by boat and by air as well as by vehicles. There is a small airport that has connecting flights to many areas in Alaska. Airplanes are as common as cars and trucks in Alaska. The unfortunate part is that there are also many tragic ends to air travel in Alaska.

Halibut Cove is also a must on the trip. The tiny hamlet lies across Kachemak Bay from Homer. The ferry *Danny J* will take you there. Halibut Cove is home to the Saltry Restaurant, which specializes in unique ways of preparing seafood. It is also home to Marian Beck's Gallery that features local artists and Diana Tillion's Gallery and Studio.

The Homer Spit is also famous for its eagles. Jean Keene, also known as "Eagle Lady" has helped in the survival rate of the eagle during the long winter months, when she feeds them with donated fish scraps every day between December and April.

AMERICAN LEGION IN HOMER

SOUTH PENINSULA HOSPITAL IN HOMER

A VERY NICE PARK IN HOMER

MARY KELLEHER ~ THE BEST BARTENDER IN HOMER

HOMER IS THE HALIBUT CAPITAL OF THE WORLD

A VERY BIG HALIBUT

Among other animals that one can see is the moose. The moose frequent the area in early spring to have their babies. It is a common sight to see them all over, including the post office. The babies are all legs and are so cute to watch as they run and jump. The mother is very attentive and it isn't a wise thing to do to get to close.

To the west of Homer, lie Cook Inlet and Mt. Augustine and Mt. Iliama, both of which are active volcanoes. Beyond Mt. Augustine is McNeil River where I went to view the brown bears. Homer is indeed a special place to visit.

There are several other towns that need mentioning, Seward, Haines, Skagway, and Hyder.

Seward lies on Resurrection Bay and is 125 miles south of Anchorage. The town was named for William H. Seward, who arranged for Alaska's purchase from Russia. It is famous for its July 4th celebration and also the Mount Marathon Race. It also holds the annual Silver Salmon Derby. Exit Glacier is about ten miles from Seward, it is one of the most accessible glaciers in Alaska and I think one of the most beautiful. The Seward Highway was designated a National Scenic Highway.

THE ALASKA RAILROAD IN SEWARD


On the trip back to Anchorage, one may be lucky to see doll sheep on the rocky cliffs or catch a glimpse of Killer or Beluga Whales feeding in Turnagain Arm.

The village of Haines is at the end of the Haines Highway from Haines Junction. It is located on the upper arm of Lynn Canal. The U.S. government established a permanent military post here in 1904, and named it Fort William H. Seward after the man who arranged for the purchase of Alaska from Russia. There is ferry service here to Skagway, which cuts off a lot of miles if you're heading for Whitehorse or East on the Alcan. Haines is home to the Alaska Chilkat Bald Eagle Preserve on the Chilkat River.

RED ~ CHECKING THE SIGHTS IN HAINES

From Haines we will go to Skagway on the ferry. Skagway lies on the north end of the Lynn Canal. Skagway is famous for the Klondike gold rush. There is so much history here. You can actually hike the Chilkoot Trail or take a train ride on the Whitepass Railway, a 3 hour trip from Skagway to White Pass Summit and return. The buildings in Skagway portray the history of the gold rush days, and offer a paradise of shopping choices. It is a striking picture to look down the city street and see an enormous cruise ship that appears to be sitting right on the street. Be sure and visit the Visitor Center for information on the vast history of this region.

SKAGWAY STREET WITH CRUISE SHIP DOCKED IN PORT

SKAGWAY SHOPPING

One area that needs mentioning is Hyder, Alaska. To reach this unique town you must travel the Cassiar Highway, due south from Watson Lake. You will come to Stewart, British Columbia first, and a couple of miles more and you will enter Hyder, Alaska. It is like going back in time, with very old buildings and dirt streets. Services are few and it makes one wonder what keeps the people here. We learned that forestry plays a big part and history has it that years ago, gold and silver were mined here. Bear Glacier is a must see on this trip. We also saw an abundant amount of bears (brown and black) along the Fish Creek area.

As you can see Brandy and Elmo continue to be our little mascots in our journey.

ELMO AND BRANDY

We often envy the eagle and its ability to soar so high and survey the landscape from many vantage points. The eagle represents what "Born Free" means.

We have made ten adventure filled journey's to Alaska and each has left us with life long memories. Our travel vehicles have varied as well.

Alaska is like a different country, it lures you there for a trip of a lifetime and then keeps calling you back again and again. It is majestic, forbidden and mysterious and it would take an entire lifetime to discover its many treasures.

We now travel in a 2003, 36 foot Monaco LaPalma with two slides and a bath and a half.

We end this story of our many adventures and we are planning another trip to Alaska in May of 2005, and consider writing a second edition to

'ALASKA ONE MORE TIME'

# Order Form

Please send_____copies of
ALASKA ONE MORE TIME

$16.95 US/$22.95 Canada
per copy
Plus S & H

NAME_____

ADDRESS_____

Shipping & handling $3.00_____

Total amount_____

Please make checks payable to R& R Enterprise
Allow 3 to 4 weeks for delivery.  Thank you

Mail to Red & Rose
c/o R & R Enterprise
5224 Kings Mill Rd.
#210
Mason, OH  45040